Praise for
The Gospel for P

D1073060

"On these pages, Tyler's creative wisdom shines, and his focus always remains on Jesus."

— **Beth & Jeff McCord, co-founders of Your Enneagram Coach, best-selling authors of *Becoming Us: Using the Enneagram to Create a Thriving Gospel-Centered Marriage***

" ... an extraordinary gift to all Enneagram fans ... . The reflections are provocative, sometimes difficult, and oftentimes liberating."

— **Marilyn Vancil, author of *Self to Lose, Self to Find: Using the Enneagram to Uncover Your True, God-Gifted Self***

"Journey through these pages to remember who you are and how to bring your best self to a world in need."

— **Dr. Drew Moser, author of *The Enneagram of Discernment: The Way of Vocation, Wisdom, and Practice***

"... thoughtful descriptions and follow-up questions are mind and heart provoking ... ."

— **Catherine Bell, founder & author, *The Awakened Company***

"*The Gospel for Peacemakers* is a soothing and powerful offering to Enneagram Nines in the Christian community."

— **Rev. Clare Loughrige, co-author of *Spiritual Rhythms for the Enneagram***

"There are books that make you *feel* better and books that make you *be* better, and this one is both. As a Peacemaker myself, I found myself nodding to every example."

— **Twyla Franz, author of *Cultivating a Missional Life***

The Gospel for Peacemakers

A 40-Day Devotional for Supportive,
Easygoing Mediators

BY TYLER ZACH

Edited by Joshua Casey, Stephanie Cross,
and Lee Ann Roberts

The Gospel For Peacemakers: A 40-Day Devotional for Supportive, Easygoing Mediators: (Enneagram Type 9)

© 2021 by Tyler Zach

Edited by Joshua Casey, Stephanie Cross, and Lee Ann Roberts

Cover design by Fruitful Design (www.fruitful.design)
Interior Design and eBook by Kelley Creative (www.kelleycreative.design)

ISBN: 9798592808128

www.gospelforenneagram.com

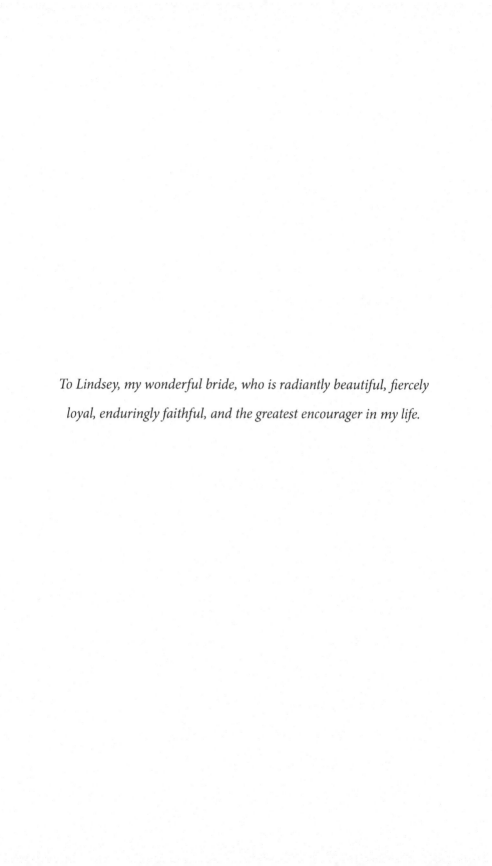

To Lindsey, my wonderful bride, who is radiantly beautiful, fiercely loyal, enduringly faithful, and the greatest encourager in my life.

Table of Contents

Foreword

WHEN JEFF AND I FIRST DISCOVERED THE Enneagram, it wasn't easy finding books written from a Christian worldview. We understood how important gospel-centered Enneagram resources could be, and that inspired us to start our business, Your Enneagram Coach. Since then, we've helped over 1,000,000 people find their Type through our free assessment, and grow through our online classes, coaching certifications, books, and now a podcast.

I'm so thankful you've picked up this devotional because that means you've decided to invest in yourself, and that is difficult for a Type 9 to do (trust me, I know, I'm also a Type 9!). The first step is often the hardest for us, and you've already accomplished that by reading these words. You may not believe it now, but your passions and your desires matter! This devotional will help you reclaim your voice.

The Enneagram is a tool that clarifies our fallen nature while also reminding us we are created in the imago Dei (image of God). When Jeff and I understood the why behind our thoughts and actions, it transformed how we looked at ourselves, our relationship with God, our marriage, our parenting, and (obviously) our careers. Taking a risk by starting a business was both exciting and terrifying. We could have easily spun out of control or run out of gas (at times we did!), but knowing the Enneagram, as seen through the lens of the gospel, kept us grounded and on track.

The world needs Type 9s. You are a great mediator, and you bring harmony to unlikely situations. You can understand all perspectives, and you always make space for everyone to have a voice and feel heard. Your quiet strength is both comforting and inspiring to others.

Like all numbers, Type 9s can have seasons of struggle. When you feel stressed, you tend to escape to a peaceful inner world, and you struggle to deal with reality as it is. The Enneagram can help you recognize when you are numbing out. You can wake up to your thoughts, feelings, and desires and bless the world with your full presence. Type 9s, we are confident this 40-day devotional will guide you toward a more confident and bold YOU.

Jeff and I are thankful the Lord has provided more gospel-centered Enneagram teachers like Tyler Zach. Whether you are new to the Enneagram or have studied it for years, we know that you'll find lasting value in this book. On these pages, Tyler's creative wisdom shines, and his focus always remains on Jesus. We're praying that God will meet you on these pages, and you will recognize your inherent value as His beloved child.

Jesus is the author and perfecter of our faith (Hebrews 12:2). He finished the great task He set out to do (John 19:30). A vital part of His ministry was to stay in alignment with His Father, and He did this by setting aside time for rest and reflection. He invites you to do the same, to come away, to separate from the crowds, and BE with Him. Remember, you are loved and valued for simply being you. You do not have to win Christ's approval. You are accepted right now as you are.

—Beth and Jeff McCord
co-founders of Your Enneagram Coach
best-selling authors of *Becoming Us: Using the Enneagram to Create a Thriving Gospel-Centered Marriage*

Introduction:

The Gospel for Peacemakers

I'M SO GLAD YOU PICKED UP THIS book because, trust me, there's a lot to affirm about you. Peacemakers are easily the most likable personality: your smile, non-threatening posture, selfless nature, and ability to pour oil on troubled waters make you well-loved. Your presence is enjoyed by all.

Here's the deal: sometimes, it doesn't feel that way. There are times when you feel like your presence doesn't matter and your contributions are questioned. That's why I wrote this book: to convince you that the world needs you. Our increasingly diverse and always divisive world needs your open, healing presence. We need someone to remind us that we are all connected, that we must take our eyes off ourselves and realize we are being grafted into something far greater.

Even though you'd prefer to stay out of the spotlight, God has written an incredible story for your life. You were not created to be a supporting cast member. God has called you to show up and create the life and world you want to wake up to tomorrow. You have so much to bring to God's great narrative, but everyone needs a little push sometimes.

Over the next 40 days I want to come alongside you to help you to grow in confidence, be more assertive and decisive, resist passive-aggressive tendencies, stop making excuses, create clear boundaries, end unhealthy relationships and enhance healthy ones, remove the leadership lid you may have placed on yourself because of fear or self-doubt, and dig up all the potential you may have buried trying to "play it safe." This devotional has just as much to do with what comes after the 40 days as it does with what you learn while reading this book. Your legacy will not be determined by what you *dream* but by what you *do*.

The Enneagram can be a helpful and necessary part of spiritual growth through self-awareness. Unlike other "personality" profiles such as *Clifton StrengthsFinder* and *Myers-Briggs Type Indicator*, the aim of the Enneagram is to uncover why we do what we do—to help us see what lies behind our strengths and weaknesses. If we use this as a diagnostic tool and allow the Bible to provide the language for our interpretation, then the Enneagram can produce great change in our lives, relationships, and work.

This is a book about Enneagram types, but don't be mistaken. Fundamentally, I'm a church planter and pastor who believes the Bible is the inspired Word of God and is sufficient for all He requires us to believe and do. That said, I *also* believe God has provided additional insights in fields such as medicine and psychology that are helpful in understanding the incredible world God has made. We must tread carefully as we draw insights from fields with limited horizons of evidence like psychology (we still have so much more to learn about the brain!). As with anything we come across in this fallible world, we can put on our gospel lens and make use of what God has provided through His common grace.

So What Makes This Book Different?

While there are other projects explaining the Enneagram, the primary aim of this book is to go deeper by applying the truth of God's Word specifically to your type over the next 40 days. If you are suspicious of the Enneagram or know someone who is, download my free resource called "Should Christians Use The Enneagram?" at gospelforenneagram.com. I pray it will help you engage with the Enneagram as a Christian, and then talk about it with others.

Before we get to the daily devotions, let's look at how the gospel both affirms and challenges the unique characteristics of your type.

The Gospel Affirms Peacemakers

God sympathizes with the worldview of a Peacemaker. This chaotic world lacks harmony and is filled with overblown egos and divisiveness. We need humble, assertive leaders to diffuse conflict by valuing all sides, seeking compromise, and building consensus. Therefore, a Peacemaker will be happy to know that the Bible affirms the following beliefs:

- **God created us to live with peace of mind in an unstable world**. "And the peace of God, which surpasses all understanding, will guard your hearts and your minds in Christ Jesus."[1]

- **God created us to coexist in harmony**. "For he himself is our peace, who has made us both one and has broken down in his flesh the dividing wall of hostility."[2]

- **God created us to be deeply connected**. "God arranged the members in the body, each one of them, as he chose. If all were a single member, where would the body be? As it is, there are many parts, yet one body."[3]

- **God created us to be includers**. "Live in harmony with one another. Do not be haughty, but associate with the lowly. Never be wise in your own sight."[4]

- **God created us to make space for everyone to be heard**. "Do nothing from selfish ambition or conceit, but in humility count others more significant than yourselves. Let each of you look not only to his own interests, but also to the interests of others."[5]

- **God created us to restore broken relationships**. "In Christ God was reconciling the world to himself, not counting their trespasses against them, and entrusting to us the message of reconciliation."[6]

- **God created us to build unity in the midst of diversity.** "I appeal to you, brothers, by the name of our Lord Jesus Christ, that all of you agree, and that there be no divisions among you, but that you be united in the same mind and the same judgment."[7]

The Gospel Challenges Peacemakers

The gospel also provides specific challenges to Peacemakers. Now we'll explore the most common lies Peacemakers believe and see how the Bible provides much

---

1   Phil. 4:7

2   Eph. 2:14

3   1 Cor. 12:18-20

4   Rom. 12:16

5   Phil. 2:3-4

6   2 Cor. 5:19

7   1 Cor. 1:10

better promises and blessings. We will move more deeply into each of these throughout the course of the next 40 days.

- **Lie #1: My presence doesn't matter.** One of the core fears of a Peacemaker is feeling *invisible or overlooked.* When you forget that God's eyes are always on you, it can lead to forgetting yourself and carrying an overly-modest "I'm nobody special" attitude. You must not give into the temptation to belittle yourself—true humility is seeing yourself as God sees you. Rather than discounting yourself and your God-given abilities, you must use them to show up in the world because you were put here for a reason.

- **Lie #2: I must go along to get along.** To gain a sense of acceptance, a Peacemaker will sacrifice their own desires and merge with or live through others. Thus, while the mental fixation of a Peacemaker is all too often *others' agendas,* glorifying God should be our highest priority. The good news is that merging with Jesus—losing ourselves in Him—actually leads to finding and becoming more of who you were meant to be. When our identity is in Christ, we are freed from people-pleasing in order to live *from* God's acceptance rather than *for* others' acceptance.

- **Lie #3: I must avoid conflict at all costs.** Another core fear for Peacemakers is *losing connection* with others. When "keep calm" becomes your motto, peacemaking will become peacefaking—denying or fleeing from conflict through the defense mechanism of *numbing* yourself. To escape the pain or minimize the tension, you'll consume food or substances or engage in routines that require little attention but provide maximum comfort. On the cross, Jesus showed us that peacemaking is active. More than the mere absence of conflict, the victory of reconciliation comes through fighting for peace by showing up and enduring discomfort.

- **Lie #4: It's not okay to assert myself.** In an attempt to not come off as pushy and risk relational disruption, Peacemakers will adopt a "play dead to stay alive" strategy. But you were not created to be a "yes man" or "yes woman"; you were made in the image of the "God who declares." As an image-bearer, you must pursue courageous transparency over insecure obscurity by declaring your convictions, speaking up for yourself, disagreeing with others, and saying no more.

- **Lie #5: I shouldn't rock the boat.** Peacemakers are wired to erase lines in the sand rather than draw them. But Jesus came to redraw the lines of His ultimate authority and our allegiance to Him. Peace has no fellowship with darkness. Sharing truth is hard because it always generates resistance—the very thing Peacemakers try and avoid at all costs. But Jesus clothed us with power and gave us all authority to call out sin, confront false religion, and protest injustice. True love has a backbone.

- **Lie #6: Good things always come to those who wait.** While patience is a virtue, it must never become an excuse. The vice of *sloth* must be turned into the virtue of *right action*. Rather than waiting for someone else to give us the life we want, we must learn to see when it is time to make a move. We're called to be doers of the Word, become zealous for good works, and work out our free gift of salvation. Love is a verb. We are partners with God, not passive-recipients when it comes to our calling and spiritual growth.

As you can see, the gospel will challenge your perception of the protagonists and antagonists in your life. In a Peacemaker's kingdom, those who are the most non-confrontational are rewarded. Your "heroes" become those who acknowledge you, ask for your opinion, and don't make demands. Likewise, your "villains" become those who call you to action, challenge you with truth, raise concerns, and persistently ask you to do something you should do but don't want to do.

However, God's kingdom will not be filled with those who kept the peace but those who fought for peace. In this place, selfishness is exchanged for stewardship so that we might hear the affirming words, "Well done, good and faithful servant."[8] In this place are those who obey without delay, risk it all rather than play it safe, and work out rather than numb out conflict. In this place, anger is turned into action, daydreams into reality, and wrestling with God into a willingness to prove how deeply we care for the relationship.

The Invitation

When Jesus Christ, the Divine All in All, entered into flawed and limited human history, He started His mission with an invitation: "The time is fulfilled, and the

---

8 Matt. 25:23

kingdom of God is at hand; repent and believe in the gospel."[9] He explained that in order to enter the good, eternally renewing life that begins well before the grave, you must do two things: believe the truth and turn from sin. Believing includes acknowledging who God is, who He says we are, and what He has done for us. Turning includes shedding our false worldview, misplaced desires, defense mechanisms, strategies we use to run and hide from God, and self-salvation efforts.

If you are ready to begin this incredible 40-day journey and accept God's invitation, then let's go! It will be an enlightening ride of rapid growth in the days to come as you become more self-aware and experience newfound freedom. You will encounter many "aha" moments as you read profound truths for your type—and maybe even learn something about the people around you. The things you learn about yourself in this book will be guaranteed to stick with you for the rest of your life.

9 Mrk. 1:15

Day 1:

It Is Well With My Soul

I have said these things to you, that in me you may have peace. In the world you

will have tribulation. But take heart; I have overcome the world.

—John 16:33

"PEACE BE WITH YOU"[2] WERE THE FIRST words Jesus spoke to His beloved disciples after rising from the dead. The first words heard from the One who had seen the other side and come back again were words of *peace*. Pause for a moment and listen to the victorious Jesus as He still speaks those powerful words over you: "Peace be with you." After overthrowing Satan and death itself, Jesus' first word was *peace*.

> When peace like a river,
>
> attendeth my way,
>
> When sorrows like sea billows roll
>
> Whatever my lot,
>
> thou hast taught me to say
>
> It is well, it is well, with my soul
>
> –Horatio Spafford[1]

---

1   Horatio Spafford, "It Is Well with My Soul," 1876, in The Baptist Hymnal, ed. Wesley L. Forbes (Nashville, TN: Convention Press, 1991), hymn 410.

2   John 20:19

Peace: the dread of death's sting has been sapped of its strength. *Peace*: the gates of Hell have been thrown down, the grave emptied. *Peace*: I have fought the battle for you, and have returned to show you the way.

God knitted the world together in peace, connecting everyone and everything together with cords of love. Peace is just as foundational as the law of gravity, the hidden presence undergirding all creation and holding things together. It's not an idealistic hope for some time without strife, but an active ingredient in the fabric of creation and its original intent. God created Eden to be warm and loving, tranquil and perfectly calm. More than lacking pain, there was a dynamic, perfect harmony between God and man, and man and woman. In the garden, man loved and was capable of loving in return.

Then it happened. One small snag in the fabric was pulled and God's peace began to unravel. The world turned cold, chaotic, and unpredictable. Adam and Eve rebelled against the God of Peace, intent on seizing for themselves the life that was offered as a free gift. Distrusting and disregarding the One who promised to guard their hearts and minds with His peace, Adam and Eve snapped the string of harmony, and discord sprang between them and the creation they were intended to steward.

> You've been given a peace that can withstand any circumstance.

We now live in a world of sin—a stubborn condition turning us from peacemakers into peacebreakers. We claim to love peace, but have a difficult time *making* it. In relationships, instead of having love and care reflected back, others intentionally or unintentionally assault our peace. Because of that reality, we are all living the life we never expected. We envision the dream cast by Eden in a world of peace, but instead exist in a world of pain.

In 1871, a prominent Chicago lawyer and Presbyterian church elder named Horatio Spafford had his world turned upside down. That year, his four-year-old son died of scarlet fever and then the Great Chicago Fire devastated his carefully crafted finances. Two years later, another tragedy struck. While crossing the

Atlantic ocean, Horatio's steamship, *Ville du Havre,* was struck by another vessel, killing 246 people, including Horatio's four daughters.[3]

It's almost inconceivable to imagine how someone could recover from such a loss, but the story doesn't end there. While traveling back across the Atlantic to be with his wife after the tragedy—across the same waters of his daughters' grave— Horatio penned the following words:

> *When peace like a river, attendeth my way,*
> *When sorrows like sea billows roll*
> *Whatever my lot, thou hast taught me to say*
> *It is well, it is well, with my soul*[4]

These words became "It Is Well With My Soul." This hymn has become the church's defiant call of hope over the last 150 years, even amidst the pain of a constantly groaning creation.

The Good News for Peacemakers is that you've been given a peace that can withstand any circumstance. This is a peace that does more than simply calm a storm; it has the power to create a vibrant spirit of wholeness where once there was emptiness and darkness. Without God, life is unpredictable and will leave you vulnerable; with God, "The peace of God, which surpasses all understanding, will guard your hearts and your minds in Christ Jesus."[5] Whenever you are tired and weary, this promise stands: "I will give you rest."[6] Like Horatio, you too can sing "It is well with my soul" in every high and low. If that is the desire of your heart, then surrender yourself to the God of Peace.

---

3   Justin Taylor, "It Is Well with My Soul," The Gospel Coalition, November 21, 2009, https://www.thegospelcoalition.org/blogs/justin-taylor/it-is-well-with-my-soul/.

4   "It Is Well With My Soul (Lyrics Video) - Audrey Assad," Churches Near Me, accessed November 15, 2020, https://church.org/2017/11/well-soul-lyrics-hymn-history/.

5   Phil. 4:7

6   Matt. 11:28

→ **Pray**

Father, You created the world in peace. My soul longs to go back to the garden to experience the world as it should be. Our sin has unraveled everything and only You can put it back together again. Thank You for sending Your Son Jesus to calm the chaos and heal the hostility. Because You've engaged the world, I know I too can engage the world with Your Spirit and without fear. Help me to do more than simply enjoy Your peace, help me to make it.

Day 1 Reflections:

How would you describe peace?

"Love around me, love below me;" Love, goodness, security; a perfect relationship with God forever.

When have you experienced a *peaceful bliss* that made you think that everything was as it should have been? Where were you? What were you doing?

Having brunch with my sister in Nashville; doing nothing on a sleepy afternoon with loved ones; snuggling with my mom and dad.

How might the knowledge that God can bring rest to your soul—no matter what life throws at you—change your engagement with the world?

I'm still learning what this means, but I know I can trust him to give me strength and peace in any situation and that he will not leave me alone.

→ **Respond**

Listen to the hymn "It Is Well With My Soul" and delight in the God of Peace.

Day 2:

A Sanctuary of Peace

Blessed are the peacemakers, for they shall be called sons of God.

—Matthew 5:9

PEACEMAKERS SPEND MUCH OF THEIR LIVES LOOKING at the world through the eyes of others, but today I want to look at *you*. Many talented and gifted people are in the world who seem to be doing great things, but God created you because the world *needs* you.

God created us as "mirrors," reflecting His heart and character to a broken and hurting world. We are truly the *imago Dei*, translating the infinite, invisible One for a finite, visible world. In the beginning, God created the heavens and earth in the context of *shalom*. This word—usually translated as "peace"—speaks to a weightier concept than the mere absence of conflict. Instead, as sociologist James Davison Hunter says, *shalom* is "a vision of order and

> You may even find that you begin ... drawing people around the cozy fire of your own spirit.
>
> –Jessica Kantrowitz[1]

---

1 Jessica Kantrowitz, *The Long Night: Readings and Stories to Help You Through Depression* (United States: Fortress Press, 2020), 156.

harmony, fruitfulness and abundance, wholeness, beauty, joy, and well-being."[2] Take a moment to reflect on each of those words. You were brought into this world precisely to usher that vision of *shalom* to the rest of us: to create a vibrant, life-giving wholeness in a world intent on death and decay.

Enneagram authors Don Richard Riso and Russ Hudson describe Peacemakers in this way:

> Nines serve as emotional anchors for people; stable and solid, they are always there when others need them. Modest, gentle, and approachable, they are sanctuaries of peace to whom others come for solace, rest, and comfort. Uncritical and un-threatening, they do not have unattainable standards either for themselves or for anyone else. They are easy to please and make few demands on anyone.[3]

They seem to say, "if you can't get along with a Peacemaker, it's not *their* fault but *yours*." Nines are so pleasant, easygoing, natural, unpretentious, honest, down to earth, and have no desire for prestige, or to impress or condemn others. They "speak with the honesty of children and the wisdom of adults" and become the kind of friend to us that fits "as comfortable as an old shoe."[4]

> God created you because the world needs you.

As a Peacemaker, you are not as easily trapped by dualistic thinking as other types. Rather, you are keenly aware that *all* people are made in the image of God, which means there is inherent goodness in every human being. Therefore, your goal is to lavish love on all people to bring out that goodness, just as Jesus reminds us that "[God] makes his sun rise on the evil and on the good, and sends rain on the just and on the unjust."[5]

Because Peacemakers don't have big egos, they don't live to make a name for themselves but rather work for the *greater good*. As Enneagram expert Beatrice

---

2 James Davison Hunter, *To Change The World: The Irony, Tragedy, and Possibility of Christianity in the Late Modern World* (New York: Oxford University Press, Inc., 2010), 228.

3 Don Riso and Russ Hudson, *Personality Types: Using the Enneagram for Self-Discovery* (HMH Books, 1996), 349-350.

4 Ibid, 351-352.

5 Matt. 5:45

Chestnut explains, "At work, Nines may expend large amounts of energy working to further other people's projects or putting time into programs that improve the quality of life at work for the organization as a whole."[6] In other words, the way you work and serve is noticeable to all because all benefit. When you step up to the plate and use your talents for the thriving of all, the *imago Dei* shines through. We see how generous God is through your generosity.

The bad news is that we all—Nines included—often forget ours and others' divine worth and calling. When this happens, *shalom* takes a back seat to chaos and conflict.

The Good News for Peacemakers is that you likely cannot live in a state of chaos and conflict for long. Your inherent desire for *shalom* will almost always rise to the surface, so your responsibility is to realize you were not meant to bring peace on your own. The world *needs* you, but it needs a healthy you. As an image-bearer of God, you have an important role to play in the unfolding plan of redemption. You must first receive this redemption through accepting Christ's offer of *shalom* for yourself in order to offer it to others.

→ Pray

Father, I praise you for Your abundant peace. In relationship with You there is harmony and wholeness, beauty and order. You've bestowed on me infinite love and worth. I want to ask You to forgive me for thinking less of myself and forgetting the ways You've gifted and empowered me. Unleash me by Your Holy Spirit to bring Your shalom to the people and places You've called me.

---

6   Beatrice Chestnut, *The 9 Types of Leadership: Mastering the Art of People in the 21st Century Workplace*, Kindle edition (Post Hill Press, 2017), 286-287.

Day 2 Reflections:

What do you enjoy about being a Peacemaker? What challenges do you face?

Which words most reflect the image of God in you? *Peaceful, harmonious, calm, fair, balanced, stable, patient, inclusive, accommodating? What others come to mind*?

Which words do you resist and judge the most in others? Biased, ambitious, aggressive, expressive, pushy, bigoted, excluding, hotheaded, unpredictable, and controlling.[7]

→ Respond

This may be tough for you, but ask someone close to you to tell how they've seen you exhibit the divine characteristics (listed in reflection question #2) in tangible ways.

---

7 Reflection questions #2 and #3 are from: Scott Loughrige, Clare M. Loughrige, Douglas A. Calhoun, and Adele Ahlberg Calhoun, *Spiritual Rhythms For The Enneagram: A Handbook for Harmony and Transformation* (Downers Grove, IL: InterVarsity Press, 2019), 37.

Day 3:

You Matter

So [Hagar] called the name of the Lord who spoke to her, "You are a God of

seeing," for she said, "Truly here I have seen him who looks after me." Therefore

the well was called Beer-lahai-roi [the well of him who lives and sees]; it lies

between Kadesh and Bered.

—Genesis 16:13-14a

No one wakes up in the morning saying, "I'm going to view myself as less-than today." But it's something that happens subconsciously as you take blow after blow for the sake of peace.

–Elisabeth Bennett[1]

WHILE SOME PEOPLE ARE FULL OF THEMSELVES, Peacemakers are typically full of anything *but* themselves. They see others as more important and will speak for them long before they stick up for themselves—often to a fault. When unhealthy, Peacemakers will completely neglect themselves or even use false modesty as a strategy.

1   Bennett, Elisabeth (@9ish_andiknowit). "We've talked this week about conflict and boundaries." *Instagram*, June 25, 2020. Accessed November 15, 2020. https://www.instagram.com/p/CB3G5-Ip7N0/

As Riso and Hudson explain,

> "Identifying themselves as Nobody Special also offers Nines a certain camouflage, an ability to blend into the background where they will not be intruded on. Their Social Role also gives them the hope that if they do not take care of themselves, others will see their self-effacing humility and rush to their side."[2]

Most often, Peacemakers simply go unnoticed and underappreciated. They can be reduced to "cogs in the machine" in an achiever society that values productivity over people.

Hagar, an Egyptian slave, is just a cog in Abraham's family machine, supporting his goals without getting anything in return. She has no other options than to simply continue serving those who take her for granted. Do you know the feeling?

After Abraham and Sarah are unable to conceive, they grow tired of waiting on God to fulfill the promise of offspring. In desperation, Sarah convinces Abraham to sleep with Hagar. To us, this might not seem like a solution for Sarah's issue, but it was common practice in the ancient world for an infertile wife to use a servant girl as a surrogate.

True humility is seeing yourself as God sees you.

If Hagar's union with Abraham produced a child, the child would legally be considered Sarah's offspring.

Sure enough, Hagar conceives, but Sarah immediately feels contempt for her. It's unclear if Hagar actually does anything to anger her mistress or if the simple fact of her pregnancy pushes Sarah over the edge. Regardless, the young, now pregnant woman, is no longer wanted. Fearing conflict, Abraham refuses to speak for Hagar (or his unborn child) and gives permission to his wife to treat Hagar as she wishes. Sarah's treatment is so bad that Hagar chooses to go on the run. Having no right or ability to defend herself, in desperation, she flees into the

---

2   Don Richard Riso and Russ Hudson, *The Wisdom of the Enneagram: The Complete Guide to Psychological and Spiritual Growth for the Nine Personality Types,* Kindle edition (New York: Bantam Books, 1999), 324.

desert. There, lost, alone, and pregnant with a child she did not ask for, she asks only for death.

Suddenly, the Angel of the Lord appears before Hagar, offering water and words of comfort, promising her descendants will be too many to count. She immediately praises God by saying, "You are *El Roi!*" meaning, "the God who sees me." Though she feels abandoned, unsupported, and invisible, "the God who sees" looks on her with love and care.

Maybe you're in a season where you believe no one sees or cares about you. You've been wondering if anyone will truly listen to, appreciate, or even pay attention to you. Perhaps you are in a dire situation not of your making but are forced to deal with anyway. Look no further than Hagar's story to be reminded that this God sees you *right now.* He says to you, "Why are you hiding? Why are you running? Come back. I see you and will be with you." Will you, like Hagar, praise *El Roi* today?

The Good News for Peacemakers is that God sees those who feel invisible. Beyond Hagar, the Bible is full of stories of those who feel forgotten and are met by God. When Hannah remains childless and feels like God isn't hearing her prayers, God listens and gives her a son named Samuel, which means, "Heard by God."[3] Jacob's wife, Leah, is constantly overlooked because she isn't as attractive as her sister, Rachel. But God sees Leah and provides.[4] When Israel begs for a king, God takes delight in anointing the unlikely and overlooked David to shepherd the people.

You matter to God. You are seen. Don't give in to despair or the temptation to belittle yourself. As the saying goes, "Humility is not thinking less of yourself, it's thinking of yourself less."[5] True humility is seeing yourself as God sees you. Part of your ongoing self-development will include learning not to discount yourself and your God-given abilities, but to use them to increase the peace and wholeness of the world.

---

3   1 Sam. 1:20

4   Gen. 29:31

5   Rick Warren, *The Purpose Driven Life: What on Earth Am I Here For?* (United States: Zondervan, 2009).

→ Pray

Father, You are El Roi. You see me even when I feel invisible. Forgive me for forgetting that You are always there. You know the number of hairs on my head and value me more than the sparrows.[6] You provide for everyday. Help me to value my personality, needs, and abilities as much as You do.

Day 3 Reflections:

How do you picture the way God is looking at you at this very moment?

_____

_____

_____

What might it look like for you to begin valuing yourself as God values you?

_____

_____

_____

How do you use the "I'm nobody special" mask to get people to rush to your side or to camouflage yourself to keep people from intruding?

_____

_____

_____

→ Respond

Being as specific as possible, write down how you think God would describe you to someone else.

6   Luke 12:7

Day 4:

Success Is In Surrender

For to us a child is born, to us a son is given; and the government shall be upon

his shoulder, and his name shall be called Wonderful Counselor, Mighty God,

Everlasting Father, Prince of Peace.

—Isaiah 9:6

DO YOU FIND IT HARD TO TELL people no? Do you feel like you are at everyone's beck and call? Being a "yes" person can leave you feeling exhausted. The desire to please others can keep you on a neverending treadmill eventually leading to insomnia and burnout. This is an unsustainable way to live.

> True peace comes not from the absence of trouble but from the presence of God.
>
> –James Hastings[1]

We may think we have control over our lives when we find success at keeping people happy and avoiding potential conflicts, but being in control is just an illusion. Life will keep coming at us. Conflicts are unavoidable. Pressure is inevitable. The only realistic option is surrender.

---

1   James Hastings, *The Great Texts of the Bible: II Corinthians and Galatians* (United States: Scribner, 1913), 402.

I'm not suggesting we leave everything up to fate. Within the Christian faith, the good news is that we don't have to give up control to an uncontrollable universe, but rather to a sovereign God who works all things for the good of those who love Him.[2]

Peace is not an impersonal force but a *person*. In the first chapter of his Gospel, the Beloved Disciple, John, describes what ancient philosophers called the *Logos*. Philosophers viewed the *Logos* as an eternal "word" or creative wisdom, but here, it was not an impersonal force—it was the person Jesus Christ. The same is true of peace. Paul said, "For [Jesus] himself is our peace."[3] Rather than leaving everything up to the unpredictability of fate, you can place yourself in the arms of a Good Shepherd who offers to know, feed, lead, and protect you even when you walk through the valley of the shadow of death.[4]

To what or whom are you surrendering in exchange for peace? Is it the universe, a religion, or a relationship? I invite you today to stop searching for the easily given peace of the changeable world, which is offered today and taken away tomorrow. Instead, find your peace in an unchanging God who is always extending the offer of life.

> Find your peace in an unchanging God who is always extending the offer of life.

Jesus once promised that those who build their house on the rock will live securely, but those who build their house on the sand will be swept away.[5] If your identity and meaning comes from surrendering to something or someone in exchange for momentary "peace," you'll soon find your self-worth (along with your peace) swept away.

The Good News for Peacemakers is that Isaiah's prophecy is fulfilled: our Prince of Peace is here. The Son of Man came to the earth and embodied divine peace as the Son of God. He was calm, patient, and understanding. He healed the sick and lame and shook the complacent out of their slumber. He stepped into

---

2   Rom. 8:28

3   Eph. 2:14

4   Psalm 23:4

5   Matt. 7:24-27

a world of chaos as an agent of active peace. Just as Peacemakers sit on top as the "crown of the Enneagram" and identify with all the types, Jesus is the true and better Peacemaker who came on a mission to identify with every type and receive a crown of thorns: "He was crushed for our iniquities; upon him was the chastisement that brought us peace."[6]

As one who loves symbols and their meaning, meditate on the symbol of the cross, which can't be reduced to words on a page or a philosophical thought in our heads. The cross is real, tangible proof of God acting decisively in human history to secure eternal peace. Don't leave your chances to fate but merge with Christ, the One who exchanged your hostility for His peace and now invites you to hide in Him as your tower of refuge in an unpredictable world. With His life flowing through you, the power to give yourself as a peacemaking offering for the world will fill you with courage you didn't know you possessed.

→ Pray

Father, I praise You that I'm in Your hands, not fate. You are my solid rock in times of trouble. Forgive my hostility toward You and for seeking temporary peace in sources that have left me feeling less safe. Thank You for sending Your Son, Jesus, to purchase my peace at great cost on the cross. By Your Holy Spirit, help me to respond to hostile people like Jesus did.

---

6 Isa. 53:5

Day 4 Reflections:

What is both freeing and frightening about putting your life in someone else's hands?

How is letting go of control to a personal God different from giving control to an impersonal universe?

Apart from God, in whom or what have you sought to secure peace?

→ Respond

Write out one thing in your life that you try to control, but need to surrender to God. How will you act decisively?

Day 5:

Settling for False Peace

They have healed the wound of my people lightly, saying, 'Peace, peace,' when

there is no peace.

—Jeremiah 6:14

"I can't breathe." George Floyd, a 46-year-old African American, repeated these words through gasps as he was slowly murdered on May 25, 2020. Derek Chauvin, a white police officer, knelt on Floyd's neck for nearly nine minutes while he was lying face down and handcuffed. Such a flagrant disregard for human life, when added to the context of a worsening global pandemic, set off a firestorm of protests and counter-protests that seemed to stretch America to the breaking point. Some protested against police brutality, racism, and a lack of accountability. People of all creeds and colors stood together, shouting for change, while others shouted back in defense of the status quo. Some, however, were silent.

> Band-aids don't fix bullet holes.
>
> –Taylor Swift[1]

In times of conflict, Peacemakers, more than any other type, will experience an inner-pull to

---

1   "Taylor Swift — Bad Blood," Genius, October 27, 2014, https://genius.com/Taylor-swift-bad-blood-lyrics.

be silent and not rock the boat. They settle for false peace, a superficial harmony based on the absence of conflict, rather than the active wholeness of *shalom*. This leads them to sweep problems under the rug, take the path of least resistance, and run away from the world's injustices.

In the Prophet Jeremiah's day, pastors and other spiritual leaders were avoiding the sin and injustices happening. Most were insulated from the dire circumstances of their countrymen, so they told everyone that the problem was no big deal and that they didn't need to worry. These agitators were violating the "peace" they valued so much. In other words, they put a band-aid on the situation. In reality, though the world began with *shalom*, it was broken and must now be fought for. The way back is not through silence and apathy, but through prophetic voice and action.

Enneagram author Ian Cron challenges Peacemakers to ask themselves whether or not their desire for peace is really (deep down) a desire to be unaffected by life.[2] In other words, is your drive for peace really just a strategy to turn down the noise and get others off your back? If so, be careful that—in your pursuit of

> Peacemakers can't receive God's peace when they are working so hard to avoid conflict.

"peace"—you don't block out God's prophetic voices calling for change. Progress and change are disruptive. The pursuit of *shalom* never feels comfortable.

Settling for false peace has its costs, not only for the world's vulnerable, but also for you. This failure to contemplate difficulty and pain will also deaden you to the good and beautiful. Plus, trying to maintain harmony in relationships can actually backfire and lead to more conflict. As Beatrice Chestnut explains, "When you don't take a firm stand or express a clear opinion, you can actually create disharmony because you can't work through the natural disagreements that occur when people work together in a conscious, direct way."[3]

Finally, fighting for false peace actually takes more effort long-term. As Riso and Hudson explain, "The irony is that average Nines must actually do something to

---

2 Ian Morgan Cron and Suzanne Stabile, *The Road Back to You*, Kindle edition (Ivp Books, 2016), 87.

3 Chestnut, *The 9 Types of Leadership*, 307.

do nothing: they must disengage themselves from anything in the environment which they perceive as a threat to their peace."[4] Peacemakers can't receive God's peace when they are working so hard to avoid conflict. One Nine put it this way: Peacemakers are like ducks who look "calm on the surface but paddling like crazy underneath."[5]

The Good News for Peacemakers comes from the great agitator, the Prophet Isaiah: "You [Lord] keep him in perfect peace whose mind is stayed on you, because he trusts in you."[6] In the midst of conflict, you can experience a supernatural, inner peace as you trust in Christ because He already purchased it for you at great cost. Though He prayed in the garden for His suffering to end and for His enemies to go away, He ultimately submitted to the Father's will and carried the cross to Calvary. Jesus showed us that the path to peace is through suffering.

Restoring *shalom* to the world requires battles, not band-aids. We must avoid anyone in this world that promises us comfort, leisure, and excessive stability without conflict. A disciple who doesn't want to carry their cross isn't really a disciple at all.

→ Pray

Father, I will trust in Your path to peace rather than anyone else's. Thank You for sending Your Son, Jesus, to suffer on the cross to restore shalom on earth. Help me to imitate His example by leaning into conflict rather than avoiding it. Give me the courage to fight to cultivate shalom rather than prevent conflict.

---

4 Riso and Hudson, *Personality Types*, 356.

5 Ian Morgan Cron, *The Road Back to You Study Guide*, Kindle edition (Ivp Books, 2016), 22.

6 Isa. 26:3

Day 5 Reflections:

When have you noticed yourself taking the path of least resistance?

_____

_____

_____

How does your desire to maintain peace at all costs cause problems for you, your relationships, and those you work with?

_____

_____

_____

How does "taking up your cross" bring clarity and set expectations for what your spiritual journey will look like?

_____

_____

_____

What would change if your primary goal shifted from "preventing conflict" to "cultivating shalom"?

_____

_____

_____

→ Respond

Rather than avoiding conflict any longer, lean in and engage by sharing what you need and want in the relationship.

Day 6:

We Are All Connected

If the whole body were an eye, where would be the sense of hearing? If the whole body were an ear, where would be the sense of smell? But as it is, God arranged the members in the body, each one of them, as he chose. If all were a single member, where would the body be? As it is, there are many parts, yet one body.

—1 Corinthians 12:17-20

DO YOU HAVE A SENSE THAT YOU are a part of something bigger than yourself—that everything is somehow connected and interdependent? Enneagram author Marilyn Vancil explains, "[Peacemakers] have a deep desire to experience the original connectivity of the human state where nothing is separated and every part is essential to the whole."[2]

> He who can no longer listen to his brother will soon be no longer listening to God either.
>
> –Dietrich Bonhoeffer[1]

1   Stephen J. Nichols, *Bonhoeffer on the Christian Life: From the Cross, for the World* (United States: Crossway, 2013), 72.

2   Marilyn Vancil, *Self to Lose Self to Find: Using the Enneagram to Uncover Your True, God-gifted Self* (New York: Convergent, 2020), 130.

While some churches focus on what you need to do as an individual, the primary metaphor the apostle Paul uses for the church is "the body," reminding us that "... we were all baptized into one body ... made to drink of one Spirit."[3] In other words, when we become Christians, we are grafted into something bigger than ourselves. Suddenly, where we once felt alone, left to bear life's weight with our own strength, ligaments and tendons have surrounded us, offering the support and the comfort of those who will walk the road with us. It's easy to see that the human body is the apex of God's creation—a marvelous machine of interconnected parts and systems working in concert to uphold a person as they walk through life.

Perhaps the perfect bodily metaphor for the Peacemakers' incredible contribution to the church is the circulatory system. Consisting of an intricate weave of vessels and capillaries, this vital system extends throughout the body, carrying oxygen, nutrients, and healing antibodies to and from our hearts into every cell in our bodies.

You help the body of Christ in this very way. You are connected deeply to the loving center of your community. You keep open lines of healthy communication flowing back and forth between every other part. You infuse empathy and support throughout every part—large or small, important or seemingly unnoticed. By just being yourself, you increase the quality of life for all through your enriching, life-giving presence.

Help your community think more inclusively and learn to embrace differences.

Paul makes a big deal about this when he explains, "If the whole body were an eye, where would be the sense of hearing? If the whole body were an ear, where would be the sense of smell?"[4] Paul goes even further by calling us to "bestow the greater honor" to those who have behind-the-scenes gifts and calls those with more "popular" or public gifts to have greater humility.[5] Regardless of the individualistic messages of our culture, we all desperately *need* each other to be healthy.

---

3   1 Cor. 12:13

4   1 Cor. 12:17

5   1 Cor. 12:23

Our increasingly diverse and always divisive world needs your open, healing presence. God created us to live with a *communal* mentality working toward a common purpose—to take the microcosm of our own ' inner harmonies and extend that into our communities. The Peacemaker's mission is to continue finding roles that allow you to forge stronger unions among people, reduce relational friction, and increase mutual understanding. Help your community think more inclusively and learn to embrace differences.[6] If you don't speak up, it might not happen.

In such an individualistic world, you must help people see the bigger picture—that connectedness implies responsibility. Ignoring or mistreating individuals will negatively affect the entire body because we are fundamentally *one*: "If one member suffers, all suffer together."[7] We all have the responsibility of loving one another as much as we love ourselves.

The Good News for Peacemakers is that Christ holds all of us together.[8] We have a good *head* on our shoulders. As Paul says, "Speaking the truth in love, we are to grow up in every way into him who is the head, into Christ, from whom the whole body, joined and held together by every joint with which it is equipped, when each part is working properly, makes the body grow so that it builds itself up in love."[9]

We are driven through sinful pride to refuse our need for God and one another. Christ came into our fractured world to bind us together, tear down the walls of hostility, and build a bridge for people of different cultures. In our Scripture's final book, we see a beautiful scene of people from every tribe, tongue, and nation gathered together in perfect unity. Remember, God has chosen you to help His people toward *that* vision.

---

6   Chestnut, *The 9 Types of Leadership*, 287-288.

7   1 Cor. 12:26

8   Col. 1:17

9   Eph. 4:15-16

→ **Pray**

Father, the intricate design of our human bodies points us to ascribe praise to a wonderful Creator. Thank You for arranging Your church in the same way. Forgive us for our self-importance, self-protection, and self-dependence that create walls and disunity. Thanks be to Jesus for tearing down those walls and uniting all things. Fill me with the Holy Spirit to be a bridge builder toward that end.

Day 6 Reflections:

Where have you noticed your desire to give everyone a voice and "bring people together"?

How does a better understanding of your gifting for connectedness provide guidance on what you should be doing?

What are some ways an individualistic mindset has negatively affected our culture and churches? How does the gospel challenge that mindset and create a better way?

→ **Respond**

Identify a barrier you've noticed that is causing relational friction between two different groups of people. Create a plan to build a bridge there.

Day 7:

Just Do It

Look carefully then how you walk, not as unwise but as wise, making the

best use of the time, because the days are evil. Therefore do not be foolish, but

understand what the will of the Lord is.

—Ephesians 5:15-17

ARE YOU PRONE TO "KILLING TIME?" WE'VE all heard, "Time is money." If you think about it, we have less control over our time than our money, don't we? It's usually possible to make more money and, once in our possession, we can choose what to do with it—whether to hoard, give, or spend.

However, time is a limited resource we are forced to spend whether we want to or not. As you read this, you are "spending time" right now. Once time is spent, you can't buy it back. It is irretrievable and, though we are unsure as to the amount

> Done is better than perfect.
>
> –Greg McKeown[1]

we are given, once it's gone, it's gone. As American poet Henry David Thoreau warned, "as if you could kill time without injuring eternity."[2]

---

1   Greg McKeown, *Essentialism: The Disciplined Pursuit of Less* (United States: Crown Business, 2014), 199.

2   Henry David Thoreau, *Walden.* (United Kingdom: Thomas Y. Crowell & Company, 1910), 8.

Our time is not our own. Christ freed us from the limits of ourselves, but in accepting His freedom, we have become "bondservants."[3] Our time now belongs to God. Our time is a gift given by God for us to steward. A steward is someone who manages someone else's assets. This means that Christians manage the time God gives us for His glory.

This is why the apostle Paul admonishes the Ephesian Christians to make the best use of their time—the days are evil, the clock is ticking. In 60 seconds you'll be one minute closer to the end of your life. A fool forgets that they are "a mist that appears for a little time and then vanishes,"[4] but a wise person numbers their days.[5] It's easy to fall into the trap of thinking that there are always more days ahead to accomplish our goals.

The underlying problem with *sloth, inaction,* or *indolence* (the Peacemakers's vice) is not primarily a result of poor time management, but poor *worship.* We always find time for what's important to us—our schedule is filled with what we love.

> Show the world who God is by what you do today.

Do you tend to put the most important things on the back burner? Peacemakers are especially prone to getting caught in the "concentric circles of procrastination" as fellow Nine, Sam Stevenson, describes it.[6] Thus, their motto flips the script of the old adage: "Don't do something; just stand there."[7]

Procrastination has its pitfalls beyond creating empty hours in the here and now. As popular author and psychologist Dr. Henry Cloud warns, "Yes, you avoid the work. That feels good at the moment. But in doing that, you have made another

---

3   1 Cor. 7:22

4   James. 4:14

5   Ps. 90:12

6   Sam Stevenson is the co-host of the Christian Enneagram podcast *Enneacast:* https://lovethyneighborhood.org/enneacast/

7   Jerome Wagner, *Nine Lenses on the World: The Enneagram Perspective,* Kindle ed. (NineLens Press, 2010).

choice as well: to have a life you hate three years from now."[8] What can we do to prevent that from happening? Listen to Cloud's empowering advice:

"Do not sit there. ... If the economy is lousy, do not wait for it to change. Gain a skill in a different field. ... Do not wait for your kids to show you respect; move towards them and find out where their heart is. ... Do not wait for your depression just to go away. Make an appointment for help. ... If you are lonely, do not wait for the phone to ring. Get out and find someone."[9]

The Good News for Peacemakers is that we can start by simply *making a move*. The temptation is to think if you just wait it out, the change you desire will happen on its own. It won't. You must make a move. Though there are always a million things you *could* do, just pick one today. As the great preacher Charles Spurgeon said, "If you stop and do nothing until you can do everything, you will remain useless."[10]

Jesus, our example and exemplar, was "spiritual" and knew when to wait, but He also lived an active, concrete example of the life of faith in flesh. We must follow His lead, see the good we can do and simply do it. As an image-bearer of the One who never stops working to bring *shalom*, show the world who God is by what you do today.

→ Pray

Father, You are a God who acts. I am here because You spoke creation into existence. I am redeemed because You sent Your Son Jesus to act on my behalf. I am born again because You sent Your Holy Spirit to awaken me from the dead. I am who I am because of Your love in action. Mount me up on eagle's wings so that I might engage the world with You today.

---

8 Henry Cloud, *9 Things You Simply Must Do to Succeed in Love and Life: a Psychologist Probes the Mystery of Why Some Lives Really Work and Others Don't* (Nashville, TN: Thomas Nelson, 2006), 75.

9 Ibid, 114-115.

10 Charles Spurgeon, *Counsel for Christian Workers* (Christian Heritage), 10.

Day 7 Reflections:

How do we see Jesus resisting the temptation to procrastinate, perfectly stewarding the short time He had on earth?

How has putting things off in the short-run caused problems in the long-run?

What are you hoping will change in your life but have been waiting for someone else to fix? What can you do today that's within your power to effect change?

→ **Respond**

Do something today that God has asked you to do, but you've been putting off.

Day 8:

Risking It All

Now the Lord said to Abram, "Go from your country and your kindred and

your father's house to the land that I will show you. And I will make of you a

great nation, and I will bless you and make your name great, so that you will

be a blessing. I will bless those who bless you, and him who dishonors you I will

curse, and in you all the families of the earth shall be blessed."

—Genesis 12:1-3

DO YOU LOVE TAKING RISKS AND VENTURING out to the unknown? As a Nine, your likely reaction to that question is to go take a nap! The great patriarch, Abraham, shows the tendencies of a Nine who was pushed into the unknown. Though he made the courageous decision to leave all he knew to follow God's call, he was actually quite risk-averse. Though he constantly sought a peaceful life, he found himself in one uncomfortable situation after another.

> Avoidance of risk is the greatest risk of all.
>
> —Henry Cloud[1]

After receiving the Divine promise "I will bless you" and the resulting mountain-top experience, a famine forces Abraham and

---

1 Cloud, *9 Things*, 36-37.

Sarah to leave their country and go to an unfamiliar land called Egypt. Heading to the Pharaoh's palace with his beautiful wife and seeing a potential conflict, he lies to Pharaoh, claiming Sarah is actually his sister. As a result, God sends a plague to Pharaoh's house and makes the situation worse. In Genesis 20, similar circumstances cause him to lie again about his wife to avoid a conflict with another king. Though God extended mercy with Abraham the first time he pulled this stunt, this time God rebukes him.

We already saw what happened when Abraham tried to appease Sarah's plan to have a surrogate son through Hagar. Appeasing man instead of God always makes the situation worse. When Sarah and Hagar get into a feud after Hagar conceives, Abram abdicates responsibility and tells Sarai, "[Hagar] is in your power; do to her as you please."[2]

> Playing it safe is too risky.

Thankfully, it's not all failure for Abraham. As the patriarch and his nephew, Lot, grow in wealth and power, a conflict arises between their herdsmen. Abraham seeks to make peace by suggesting they both go their own ways. In typical Peacemaker fashion, Abraham defers to his nephew and lets him pick where he wants to go first.

When God resolves to destroy the evil cities of Sodom and Gomorrah, where Lot and his family settled down, Abraham finally steps into his role as mediator and negotiates with God on behalf of the people. Though the cities weren't spared, most of Abraham's relatives were able to escape.

Abraham also displays great faith in his willingness to put aside his desire for a legacy by following God's command to sacrifice Isaac, the only beloved son between him and Sarah. Abraham simply acts in faith and God (of course) provides a ram as a substitute sacrifice for Isaac's life. Therefore, Abraham calls the name of that place, "The Lord will provide."[3]

The Good News for Peacemakers is that the "God of Abraham" is *our* God too. We have the same access to the abundant patience and mercy Abraham receives.

---

2 Gen. 16:6

3 Gen. 22:14

As we look at this brief bio of Abraham, we see a God who is comfortable giving perfect promises to imperfect people. Though Abraham stumbled throughout his life, he will always be known for *risking it all*. When God asks him to leave his comfortable homeland, we see him *go*. When God asks him to sacrifice his son Isaac, we see him *go*. Through his faith-filled yes, God launched a plan to bless every tongue, tribe, and nation.

Do you see? Playing it safe is too risky. There's too much at stake *not* to follow God into the unknown. It won't be comfortable, and it won't be easy. It might not be the life you were expecting, but it'll be a story that inspires your descendants and disciples for generations to come.

➜ Pray

Father, I praise You for being trustworthy. With You there are no risks, for everything You ask me to do is a part of Your perfectly thought-out plan. As someone who is prone to comfort and security, free me to be a risk-taker like Jesus who risked it all on the cross to accomplish Your Will. Like Abraham, let my life be one of complete dependence on You.

Day 8 Reflections:

What blessings are you experiencing right now that are a result of someone else taking a risk?

_____

_____

_____

_____

What are you willing to give up if God asks you to pack up and move?

_____

_____

_____

What's the worst that could happen if you risked it all to follow God's call? What's the best thing that could happen?

_____

_____

_____

_____

→ Respond

Write a 50-word personal mission statement that will help you prioritize your future pursuits.

Day 9:

Rock the Boat

For am I now seeking the approval of man, or of God? Or am I trying to please

man? If I were still trying to please man, I would not be a servant of Christ.

—Galatians 1:10

ONE OF THE TELLTALE SIGNS OF A Peacemaker is the "yes nod." You know what I mean—it starts with a friend passionately sharing an opinion that we disagree with or a boss asking us to do something we don't want to do. Inside, without even having to think about it, we feel our gut saying no, but for some odd reason, our head begins to nod yes, giving the other person the impression that we are totally on board with them. Have you had this happen before? (I see you smiling.)

Peacemakers have a laissez-faire attitude about life: they go with the flow, "go along to get along," and are the first to give the

> There are always a lot of people whose motto is "Don't rock the boat." They are so afraid of rocking the boat, that they stop rowing. We can never get ahead that way.
>
> –Harry S. Truman[1]

---

1 "Commencement Address at Howard University," The Truman Library, accessed November 13, 2020, https://www. trumanlibrary.gov/library/public-papers/169/commencement-address-howard-university.

cliche advice, "let go and let God." They generally have a conservative inclination not to rock the boat. One Peacemaker described her experience this way:

> "My mother was alcoholic and had a volatile temper, so a lot of my energy as a child was directed to keeping out of the way and not rocking the boat. In this way I learned to stand on the sidelines of life and be accommodating to the needs of other people. I was afraid I wouldn't be loved if I asserted myself. I chose to live my life in a more inward way, which was actually very rich to me, without confronting other people."[2]

Peacemakers are cherished by all because they are such good listeners, even in the midst of disagreement. This humility is a true gift, but the people-pleasing yes nod can backfire. Your "I don't want to be selfish" disposition can end up hurting you and others, leading you to bend the truth, go against your values, or simply apologize more than you should. You shouldn't have to be sorry for being you; rather than *suppressing* yourself, you should be *expressing* yourself. God has given you the power to be assertive—to speak up for yourself, disagree with others, and say no more.

> Rather than *suppressing* yourself, you should be *expressing* yourself.

One of the best biblical examples of this was John the Baptist. His ministry is kicked off, not with an inspirational book, but an unpopular call to repentance. When the religious authorities pay a visit, he courageously challenges their self-serving codes of holiness and points out their misuse of spiritual authority.

John challenges the ruling authorities of his day, even up to King Herod. When John stands up to the king, he is thrown in prison. Some time later, John is unjustly beheaded after the weak and wicked king promises his daughter that she can have anything she wants. John's bravery in the face of such high stakes shows a trusting heart willing to go to any lengths to speak the truth.

John's life shows us that it's possible to be *humbly* assertive. He challenges the status quo and points people to the mighty Savior, Jesus, "whose sandals I am not

---

2 Riso and Hudson, *The Wisdom*, 317.

worthy to carry."³ He did not live for the approval of man, but for God alone, to bring His people to repentance.

The Good News for Peacemakers is that you can rock the boat if Jesus is in it. When we seek to please others and give them the key to our value, we will never find rest. However, as servants of Christ, our self-worth is secure. This frees us to speak out and talk about our desires, convictions, and beliefs—even at great risk. With Christ's affirming presence, we will begin to ask for things even if we think others will say no. We will push back when something doesn't sit right in our soul. We will publicly defend ourselves or others who are mistreated. We will also pursue our own goals and careers rather than always going along with what others want for us. So don't be afraid; go rock the boat today!

→ Pray

Father, empower me to challenge the status quo to bring You glory. Forgive me for giving into the temptation to people-please. I want to be a servant of Christ and point people to Him even if it costs me something. As your servant John said of Jesus, "He must increase, but I must decrease."⁴ Give me the courage to let my yes be my yes and my no be my no.⁵

---

3   Matt. 3:11

4   John 3:30

5   Matt. 5:37

Day 9 Reflections:

What values do you have that go against the status-quo?

_____

_____

_____

_____

What do you fear will happen if you become a more assertive person?

_____

_____

_____

_____

What expectations do the people in your life have of you? What would happen if you became convinced that pleasing God meant going in a different direction?

_____

_____

_____

_____

➜ Respond

Resist the people-pleasing temptation today by saying no to something small or taking a stand for something you value.

Day 10:

Numbing Out

And they brought [Jesus] to the place called Golgotha (which means Place of

a Skull). And they offered him wine mixed with myrrh, but he did not take it.

And they crucified him and divided his garments among them, casting lots for

them, to decide what each should take. And it was the third hour when they

crucified him.

—Mark 15:22-25

ON APRIL 15, 1912, THE WELL-KNOWN LUXURY ship *The Titanic* sank in the North Atlantic Ocean after hitting an iceberg. Of the 2,240 passengers, more than 1,500 people died in this historical disaster.[2] As you can imagine, being on that sinking ship would have been incredibly traumatic. Beginning to think of the death that awaited them, the passengers asked the bandmaster to play music to soothe their souls. Officers

> The child is grown
>
> The dream is gone
>
> And I have become
>
> Comfortably Numb
>
> –Pink Floyd, "Comfortably Numb"[1]

---

1   "Pink Floyd — Comfortably Numb," Genius, November 30, 1979, https://genius.com/Pink-floyd-comfortably-numb-lyrics.

2   History.com Editors, "Titanic," History.com (A&E Television Networks, November 9, 2009), https://www.history.com/topics/early-20th-century-us/titanic.

from the RMS Carpathia who spoke with *The Titanic* survivors after, reported that the band played a hymn to calm the panic-stricken passengers.[3]

Peacemakers often employ similar strategies when their lives begin to sink and painful feelings creep up. Just as *The Titanic* passengers turned to music to drown out the panic, Peacemakers also "tell their inner orchestra to play louder while their ship is sinking."[4]

This defense mechanism of the Peacemaker is called *narcotization.* When life becomes too difficult or uncomfortable to handle, you turn down the volume on your feelings, desires, and preferences so that "nothing gets to you." You can tell you are "emotional numbing" when you lose interest in activities you used to enjoy, feel distant or "flat," have difficulty experiencing positive feelings, and start preferring isolation over being with others.[5]

> Our Savior is better than any sedative.

One Peacemaker describes his experience this way:

"At my worst, I feel numb. Not even really depressed, just numb. The smallest things can feel like an enormous effort. Long stretches of time can pass by while I simply stare out the window and think, or crash in front of the TV and channel surf. Time simply stops. It's like becoming a zombie. I can still function in terms of going to work and appearing friendly, but inside I'm feeling completely shut down. There is a sense of hopelessness about finding a direction in life."[6]

Can you relate? Numbing yourself is more than doing nothing. It also includes doing familiar activities or daily routines that provide comfort but require little attention or depth of experience. Many things—from binge-watching, social media, and video games, to vacations, food, alcohol, or even gardening—can be a means to this end. None of these are inherently bad, but when used to deaden experience and engagement with life, they become harmful.

---

3   Steve Turner, *The Band that Played On* (Nashville, TN: Thomas Nelson, 2011), 194.

4   Cron and Stabile, *The Road Back to You*, 82-83.

5   Sara Lindberg, "What Is Emotional Numbing?," Verywell Mind, April 4, 2020, https://www.verywellmind.com/emotional-numbing-symptoms-2797372.

6   Riso and Hudson, *The Wisdom*, 326.

Numbing does not always look slothful, either. A Peacemaker may spend a significant amount of time working out or at the office, but the true aim is not productivity or growth. Instead, the goal is to numb oneself from both pain and priorities. Ultimately, numbing out only puts a band-aid on the problem. As Enneagram teacher Helen Palmer says, a Peacemaker "replaces essential needs with unessential substitutes."[7] Our substitutes are insufficient for dealing with the root issues.

Jesus was tempted by the devil to find relief from physical hunger in the wilderness. The accuser said, "If you are the Son of God, command these stones to become loaves of bread." But Jesus replied, "It is written, 'Man shall not live by bread alone, but by every word that comes from the mouth of God.'"[8] Satan tried offering a substitute to numb Jesus' pain and reduce the experience of His fast, but Jesus chose to address His more essential spiritual need: preparing for the difficult road ahead.

On the cross, Jesus was offered wine mixed with myrrh, a narcotic sedative used in that day to ease the excruciating pain of crucifixion. He declined this opportunity to sedate Himself, instead choosing a clear and present mind even in the midst of His greatest pain.

The Good News for Peacemakers is that our Savior is better than any sedative. None of us will likely be called to offer our lives, but we will still feel the urge to numb our experience of the world, blocking out the present with any number of distractions. Rather than *deadening* your senses to stay alive, the Father offers *strength* with power through Christ and His Holy Spirit, so that you can be fully *you* in every moment. The next time you feel like you are sinking, turn up the music of the gospel and draw from His unending well of peace.

---

7   Helen Palmer, *The Enneagram in Love and Work: Understanding Your Intimate and Business Relationships* (Harper-One, 2010), 224.

8   Matt. 4:3-4

→ Pray

Father, I cannot live on bread alone, but by Your words. You are a fountain of life for all who believe. With You I can be fully alive and have the abundant life Jesus came to bring. Without You, I lose myself and become dead inside. Forgive me for numbing myself with useless substitutes. As am I healed by You, the Great Physician, enable me to bring my full self to the world.

Day 10 Reflections:

What do you do or where do you go to numb out?

What need or challenge is going unmet by numbing yourself rather than facing the issue head on?

What goals are you sacrificing right now for the comfort of doing nothing?

→ Respond

Develop a support network of people who can help you when they spot the signs of numbing out in your life.

Day 11:

I Will Never Leave You

He has said, "I will never leave you nor forsake you." So we can confidently say,

"The Lord is my helper; I will not fear; what can man do to me?"

—Hebrews 13:5b-6

HOW DO YOU FEEL WHEN SOMEONE IS angry with you? No one enjoys the knowledge (or fear) that another is displeased with them. Since humanity initially lived as a tribal species, we have feared ending up on the wrong side of the group, and the fear of being cut out of the community can be paralyzing. As Helen Palmer points out, "anger equals separation."[2] For the Peacemaker, then, relational separation must be avoided at all costs. In desperate situations, we may even find ourselves retreating from our own feelings and values, saying things like, "This is *your* team. I'm here for you, please don't be upset with me."

> The right people won't leave you when you tell them no.
>
> —Alison L. Bradley[1]

1   Alison L. Bradley (@9ish_andiknowit), "A few years ago, the Lord gave me 'boundaries' as one of my words of the year." *Instagram*, June 23, 2020. Accessed November 15, 2020. https://www.instagram.com/p/CBySf95pZkU/.

2   Palmer, *The Enneagram in Love and Work*, 224.

Kahneman and Tversky's Nobel Prize-winning findings on "loss aversion" claim that the psychological pain of *losing* is twice as powerful as the pleasure of *gaining*.[3] We will burn hours and calories to keep the boat from rocking rather than risk being set adrift. Think for a moment: *Do you work harder avoiding the loss of a relationship or toward the growth and strengthening of new ones?*

This fear is real. We say to ourselves, "If I tell them what I really feel, won't they get upset? What if they don't listen or make me feel guilty? What if I regret it?" With these fears rolling around in our heads, it's easy to see why we give up and say, "I'll just keep it to myself. Better to keep everyone blissfully ignorant than have a confrontation."

Scripture defines the "fear of man" as the desire to please human beings over God when they have the power to shame, reject, or threaten us. Again, this fear of losing community is deeply embedded in our psyches. The Book of Proverbs warns that when fear becomes our primary motivator, it will become a *trap*, causing us to second-guess all of our decisions, eventually resulting in a sort of paralysis.[4]

> Pleasing others eventually causes massive displeasure with yourself.

Molding our decisions after what others *might* do is always a short-term gain, long-term loss scenario; it is not a sustainable way to live in community. Pleasing others eventually causes massive displeasure with yourself, just as stuffing your true feelings will cause you to sacrifice your opinions, values, and judgements. It *may* help you hold onto a relationship a little longer, but you will be miserable— and that cannot be hidden forever. Eventually, the effort to hide and relationally disengage may actually become a "self-fulfilling prophecy," eroding intimacy and eventually creating further loss and separation.[5]

---

3   "Prospect Theory: An Analysis of Decision under Risk," accessed November 18, 2020, https://www.jstor.org/stable/1914185.

4   Prov. 29:25

5   Riso and Hudson, *The Wisdom*, 326.

Brené Brown notes that someone in pursuit of real intimacy says, "I'm willing to put the problem in front of us rather than between us."[6] This kind of love leans *in* rather than *away*. If the other party responds poorly, that's on them. *They* are responsible for *their* response, not you. Please hear this: If you share what you believe to be *right*, their reaction doesn't automatically make you *wrong*. Their anger doesn't decide the verdict.

The Good News for Peacemakers is that no matter how many relationships you have or lose, God promises to never leave you. God has provided you with a never-ending connection with Him for as long as you live.[7] This connection is guaranteed by the One who was completely forsaken and cried out, "My God, my God, why have you forsaken me?"[8] Christ went before us, showing through His own body that nothing could separate us from God's love, so that we can now say, "My God, My God, thank You for adopting me as your own." All tension and discord between you and God has been done away with, there is now only peace. Your name is written on His heart and on His hands[9]—He will not forget about you.

When your heart is filled with awe and overwhelmed by this good news, it means that you can live *from* God's acceptance rather than *for* others' acceptance. You can share the real *you* and be bold in your relationships. Knowing that God is on your side, you won't have to ask the question, "What are people going to say?" Rather, you can say with the Psalmist, "The Lord is my helper; I will not fear; what can man do to me?"[10]

---

6   Brené Brown, *Dare to Lead: Brave Work. Tough Conversations* (United States: Random House Publishing Group, 2018), 198.

7   McCord, *The Enneagram Type 9*, 34.

8   Matt. 27:46

9   Isa. 49:16

10   Heb. 13:6

→ **Pray**

Father, remind me that fearing You is the beginning of knowledge, but that fear is based on Your love and power. Forgive me for the ways I allow others to control me. By Your Spirit, empower me to speak the truth, live out my values, and choose Your direction without the fear of disappointing people. I know that whatever happens in my earthly relationships, nothing will be able to separate me from Your love.

Day 11 Reflections:

What role has the "fear of man" played in your life?

What is really driving your desire to be nice to everyone?

How does the gospel free you from the fear of being on the receiving end of strong emotions?

→ **Respond**

Make it a goal to tell someone no today or to speak up for yourself.

Day 12:

Setting Boundaries

Keep your heart with all vigilance, for from it flow the springs of life.

—Proverbs 4:23

DOES IT EVER FEEL LIKE PEOPLE ARE invading your space? In the physical world, boundaries like fences and signs are helpful because they define where our property ends and where someone else's begins. Similarly, God created boundaries for our souls.

Henry Cloud teaches that boundaries define what is "me" and what is "not me"—where I end and someone else begins. Boundaries show us where our responsibilities lie—what we do and do not have authority over. Boundaries keep us from becoming doormats others use to control areas of our lives that aren't theirs.[2] Gandhi put it this way: "I will not let anyone walk through my mind with their dirty feet."

> The way to true peace does not come from me absorbing all the blows.
>
> –Alison L. Bradley[1]

---

1 Alison L. Bradley, (@9ish_andiknowit). "This spring, I taught a Sunday School class (to adults) on conflict." Instagram, June 24, 2019. Accessed November 15, 2020. https://www.instagram.com/p/BzG131Blj7s/?igshid=a9hodvn7s7r6

2 "What Are Healthy Boundaries?," Boundaries Books, accessed November 16, 2020, https://www.boundariesbooks.com/pages/what-are-healthy-boundaries.

The advice Peacemakers need to give themselves to do every day is: *put your foot down*. As Alison Bradley says, "No explanations or apologies are necessary for saying no."[3] There are many people in this world who want to be all up in your business, but the wisdom of Proverbs tells us, "Keep your heart with all vigilance, for from it flow the springs of life."[4]

Setting boundaries, like saying no to good people or exciting opportunities, may feel very selfish. As Cloud clarifies, boundaries are not about *selfishness* but about *stewardship*.[5] Setting boundaries protects the time and resources God has given us to leverage for His glory.

Who are you allowing to come into your "fence" and intrude on your time, decision-making, and priorities? Jesus limited His exposure to destructive people and so should we. Giving in to someone who is unhealthy may feel like a win in the moment if it successfully wards off

> You were not created to be a prisoner to the expectations of others.

an angry response. However, wisdom warns, "if you deliver him, you will only have to do it again."[6] Therefore, don't train others to get what they want from you; appeasing only enables unhealthy behavior and makes us feel like life-long hostages.

Healthy boundaries may sound like:

- "You often ask me at the last minute. I'll need more time to do what you asked."
- "Mom and Dad, I love you, but I can't be the mediator in your marriage."
- "If you text or email me while I'm on my day off, I won't respond."
- "I'm not okay with you talking about that person without you speaking to them first."

---

3   Alison L. Bradley, (@9ish_andiknowit). "This question came because several of our recent wins have mentioned not apologizing." *Instagram*, December 19, 2019. Accessed November 15, 2020. https://www.instagram.com/p/CBV3tH-9JVj0/.

4   Prov. 4:23

5   "Am I Being Selfish When I Set Boundaries?," Boundaries Books, accessed November 16, 2020, https://www.boundariesbooks.com/blogs/boundaries-blog/am-i-being-selfish-when-i-set-boundaries.

6   Prov. 19:19

To execute a boundary well, state why the boundary is important to you, point out when or how they have violated it, share how the violation made you feel, explain what you are prepared to do, and then follow through! While some people will feel sadness that they have violated your autonomy and will amend their ways, some will not. If not, Cloud says the goal is to "convert them from being controlling to being frustrated." For example, "I am sorry it is so frustrating to you that I am making this choice. I hope you can accept that I still care about you even though I have decided to do this for me."[7]

The Good News for Peacemakers is that while we can't control the behavior of others, we can limit our exposure to those behaviors. This may frustrate them, but it will save us from their toxicity or unnecessary neediness. You were not created to be a prisoner to the expectations of others, or to wait on them indefinitely to the detriment of your own life. When the Psalmist felt vulnerable and overwhelmed, he cried out, "My refuge and my fortress, my God, in whom I trust."[8] Take a hold of these words today and look to Jesus who is your hiding place, the One who will protect you on all sides. Because He loves you, you don't have to be afraid. Remember that setting boundaries will not *end* healthy relationships, but *enhance* them.

➡ Pray

Father, You are good and my safe place in times of trouble. I find refuge under the shadow of Your wings. Help me to love myself as You love me. As Your steward, enable me to set better boundaries. Let my yes be yes and my no be no.

---

7   Cloud, *9 Things You Simply Must Do*, 231-232.

8   Ps. 91:2

Day 12 Reflections:

Where do you observe healthy boundaries in your life?

_____

_____

_____

_____

Who are the "unsafe" people in your life? What makes them seem unsafe to you?

_____

_____

_____

What are some healthy emotional and physical boundaries you can set with your partner, parents/in-laws, and friendships both at home and in the workplace?

_____

_____

_____

→ Respond

Read the book _Boundaries: When to Say Yes, How to Say No to Take Control of Your Life_ by Henry Cloud and John Townsend and talk about it to someone as a way to continue the work of self-care.

Day 13:

Turn Anger Into Action

In the temple he found those who were selling oxen and sheep and pigeons, and

the money-changers sitting there. And making a whip of cords, he drove them

all out of the temple, with the sheep and oxen. And he poured out the coins of

the money-changers and overturned their tables. And he told those who sold

the pigeons, "Take these things away; do not make my Father's house a house of

trade." His disciples remembered that it was written, "Zeal for your house will

consume me."

—John 2:14-17

It's okay to feel things deeply and have big emotions. They make you human, not a burden.

–Alison L. Bradley[1]

OF ALL TYPES, PEACEMAKERS ARE EASILY THE most likeable. Your easy smiles, gentleness, listening ears, non-threatening posture, and "what you see is what you get" personality is contagious.

---

1   Alison L. Bradley (@9ish_andiknowit), "For so many of us, we have believed that the way to peace is feeling calm or happy." *Instagram*, June 9, 2020. Accessed November 15, 2020. https://www.instagram.com/p/CB3G5-Ip7N0/.

I love being around my Peacemaker friends for those reasons and do not want them to change.

Enneagram teacher Ian Cron points out that Nines may "often overattach to and enjoy their reputation for being the good guy or the nice girl."[2] To keep up this image, strategies are put in place to keep your anger in the closet—and that's not just metaphorical. Grammy-award winning singer Amy Grant told Cron on his Typology Podcast that the closet was literally her place to go and scream at the top of her lungs.[3]

Peacemakers must be more attuned to their anger. Cron notes, "Nines are out of touch with the good side of anger, the part that inspires, drives change, moves things along and gives them courage to stand up for themselves. When you're unplugged from this side of anger, you become lethargic and dreamy."[4]

Though expressing anger is frowned upon in most church circles, it's not always sinful. God did not say that anger is *never* allowed, but rather, "Be angry and do not sin."[5] Meaning, you must find positive outlets to express the natural feeling of anger. *Righteous anger* is different from *unrighteous anger* in two important ways. First, righteous anger is *God-centered*—triggered by the same things that anger God, such as injustice and hypocrisy. Second, righteous anger is *controlled*—expressed in planned, often prophetic

> Jesus has given us an example and all authority on heaven and earth to call out sin, confront false religion, protest injustice, and tell the wolves in sheep's clothing where to go.

ways. Though Jesus storming the temple with His make-shift whip of cords is often portrayed as Jesus losing His temper, a better reading reveals this as a planned act to make a prophetic point. Out of *holy* love for the church, Jesus

---

2   Cron and Stabile, *The Road Back to You*, 76.

3   Ian Morgan Cron, interview with Amy Grant, *What's Your Stance? Part 2, feat. Amy Grant (Enneagram 9) [S02-029]*, podcast audio, February 14, 2019, https://www.typologypodcast.com/podcast/2019/07/02/s02-028/amygrant-hs7w3

4   Cron and Stabile, *The Road Back to You*, 67.

5   Eph. 4:26

turns His inner anger into righteous action by driving out the money-hungry opportunists that were keeping people distant from God.

Like Jesus, if you are able to find your passion against what angers the heart of God, it can be redirected to constructive purposes. Where would the world be without the likes of Frederick Doulgass and Sojourner Truth, or Susan B. Anthony, and William Wilberforce—those who passionately sought to right the wrongs of their times and places?

Peacemakers are the original "people persons," the definition of biblical shepherd-leaders, often finding themselves in teaching, mentoring, or counseling roles. However, we often forget the tool God puts in the hand of every shepherd: a staff. A shepherd's staff is used for two primary reasons: protecting the sheep from predators and correcting those who wander off. As a disciple maker, you'll need a staff to both protect and correct those whom God entrusts to you. Even the nicest shepherd will be ineffective if they don't use a staff.

A staff was a shepherd-leader's "power" tool. Moses felt powerless to lead God's people to better pastures until he received his staff. Like Moses, do you feel unqualified to assert yourself as a leader? Remember to pick up your staff: Jesus has given us an example and *all* authority on heaven and earth to call out sin, confront false religion, protest injustice, and tell the wolves in sheep's clothing where to go.

The Good News for Peacemakers is that you have permission to be righteously angry. We worship a "God who feels indignation every day"[6] toward evil and injustice, so we can too. As sons and daughters, we aren't afraid of God's anger, but comforted by it. We can lay down in green pastures and walk beside still waters because our Shepherd carries a staff. As the Psalmist says, "Even though I walk through the valley of the shadow of death, I will fear no evil, for you are with me; your rod and your staff, they comfort me."[7] Expressing your anger outwardly like Jesus did may feel awkward at first, and you won't always get it right. As you pick up His staff, you'll learn how to wield it, watching how it brings peace and security to those under your care.

---

6 Ps. 7:11

7 Ps. 23:4

→ Pray

Father, I praise You for being my Good Shepherd, who daily provides for and protects me. Forgive me for numbing myself to the evil and injustices around me. Though You've called me to storm the temple, I've neglected my responsibility and have turned a blind eye toward sin and pain. Replace my apathy with zeal. Help me to pick up my staff and exercise Your power and authority today.

Day 13 Reflections:

Why does anger make you uncomfortable?

_____

_____

_____

Which of these injustices makes you most angry and why: abuse, violence, illness, betrayal, addiction, poverty, racism, or abandonment? What else would you add to this list?

_____

_____

_____

How can you channel that anger for constructive purposes?

_____

_____

_____

→ Respond

Keep an anger journal to begin tracking the causes and consequences of your anger.

Day 14:

Turn Daydreams Into Reality

Then I said to them, "You see the trouble we are in, how Jerusalem lies in ruins with its gates burned. Come, let us build the wall of Jerusalem, that we may no longer suffer derision." And I told them of the hand of my God that had been upon me for good, and also of the words that the king had spoken to me. And they said, "Let us rise up and build." So they strengthened their hands for the good work.

—Nehemiah 2:17-18

HAVE YOU EVER BEEN CAUGHT DAYDREAMING? I get caught so often that my son jokingly asks me, "Are you in 'Ty-land' again?" In grade school, I daydreamed so much my teacher worried I had hearing problems. After a school-mandated trip to the ear doctor, my teacher was surprised to learn my hearing was quite excellent after all.

> If you can dream it,
> you can do it.
> —Tom Fitzgerald[1]

1 This quote, often attributed to Walt Disney, was written by Imagineer Tom Fitzgerald specifically for the Horizons attraction at Epcot (https://d23.com/ask-dave/krystina-avondale-arizona-2/).

The world needs dreamers, and it needs those who can turn dreams into reality. In 1901, a young boy named Walter was born on the northwest side of Chicago. Walter grew up spending most days "in his own head," often putting his dreams into pictures. He took his first job as a commercial illustrator at the age of 18 and went on to become perhaps the most famous animator, voice actor, and film producer ever. "Walt" Disney pioneered the American animation industry and won a record 22 Oscars. His imagination was the springboard for the most popular amusement park in the world and one of the most dominant businesses in history.[2]

But he didn't do it on his own.

Did you know that Walt is said to have been a Peacemaker? You won't be surprised after hearing Riso and Hudson describe this imaginative type:

> Your legacy will not be determined by what you *dream* but by what you *do*.

"Healthy Nines supply the personality types with a vision of the magic of the world. They have a way of looking at the world through innocent eyes. Their mythological imagination recalls the consciousness of childhood in which everything seemed to glow with enchantment. ... Nines have an affinity for nonverbal communication. They are at home in the world of pictures and symbols, and they often tend to think in colors and impressions rather than in words."[3]

Nines make this world a more enchanting one, but the constant challenge will always be turning daydreams into reality. Look around you. Everything you see— artwork, televisions, homes, parks, computers—were once dreams that resided in someone else's mind. But all of those dreamers needed someone to take the dreams out of their heads and make them real.

Your legacy will not be determined by what you *dream* but by what you *do*. Dreamers cannot change the world on their own—they need doers to come alongside. Although Walt Disney was perceived to be a Type A leader, those who knew him said he was shy, self-deprecating, and insecure about his abilities. Walt

---

2 "Walt Disney." Biography.com. A&E Networks Television, August 21, 2020. https://www.biography.com/business-figure/walt-disney.

3 Riso and Hudson, *Personality Types*, 350-351.

was able to accomplish so much because of an older, business-savvy brother, Roy, who helped turn Walt's dream into reality.[4]

God's people, the Israelites, are taken into captivity in Babylon because of their disobedience and faithlessness, but decades later, they are released to make the trek back home. Nehemiah, the cupbearer to Persian Emperor Artaxerxes, is a faithful follower of Yahweh. Back home, the returned Jewish people rebuild Solomon's Temple under the direction of the scribe Ezra, but Jerusalem remains vulnerable because of the walls that were not rebuilt after the Babylonians tore them down. Nehemiah wept over the state of the holy city and began dreaming up a solution.

The challenges of rebuilding a wall are many. Nehemiah has no materials, no money, no freedom, and no authority. Enemies from without and detractors from within pose trouble at every point, but through grit, determination, and a strong will, Nehemiah sees the walls of Jerusalem rebuilt.

Have you ever felt discouraged as you looked at all the obstacles standing in the way of your dream? Have you ever felt hopeless because you felt like you didn't have the right personality or talents?

The Good News for Peacemakers is that God, who brought the world from His mind into existence *ex nihilo* (out of nothing), will do the same for you. As Pastor Andy Stanley says, "What God originates, He orchestrates."[5] After praying, Nehemiah brought the plight of his people before the Emperor and, to his amazement, this foreign king "granted me what I asked, for the good hand of my God was upon me."[6] Moses felt the same way about his impossible mission until God gave him the help of his brother Aaron. Remember, you have what it takes because you have God and His unlimited resources.

---

4   "Walt Disney." Biography.com. A&E Networks Television, August 21, 2020. https://www.biography.com/business-figure/walt-disney.

5   Brian Orme, "15 Quotes from Andy Stanley #Catalyst14 Opening Session," ChurchLeaders, November 26, 2014, https://churchleaders.com/daily-buzz/176593-15-quotes-from-andy-stanley-catalyst14-opening-session.html.

6   Neh. 2:8

→ Pray

Father, with merely a word You spoke the cosmos into existence. When Your Word goes out, it does not return empty.[7] Help me to trust You as the One who grants us our heart's desires and fulfills all our plans.[8] Because I am fearfully and wonderfully made, and You have poured out Your Spirit on me, give me the courage to declare my God-given dreams into existence.

Day 14 Reflections:

What childhood dreams have you pushed aside that need to be lived out?

As you look around, what breaks your heart? What "unfinished" plans might God be calling you to?

What fears, doubts, or obstacles regarding your dreams do you need to surrender to the Lord and trust Him with?

→ Respond

Write down your goals and dreams. Start working toward something that seems impossible without divine intervention.

---

7   Isa. 55:11

8   Ps. 20:4

Day 15:

Fan Into Flame Your Gifts

I am reminded of your sincere faith, a faith that dwelt first in your grandmother

Lois and your mother Eunice and now, I am sure, dwells in you as well. For this

reason I remind you to fan into flame the gift of God, which is in you through

the laying on of my hands, for God gave us a spirit not of fear but of power and

love and self-control.

—2 Timothy 1:5-7

IF YOU HAVE EVER BEEN CAMPING, THEN you're probably accustomed to starting fires (or watching your "outdoorsy" friend do it). Dried leaves or twigs are laid down to kindle the fire, followed by increasingly larger sticks and logs. Once the fire is ablaze, you can finally get to the good part—sitting under the stars and soaking up a good conversation. All too soon, the once-roaring flames begin to die. Rather than start the process all over again, all that's needed is

> Ask God's blessing on your work. But don't ask him to do it for you.
>
> —Flora Robson[1]

---

1 Cloud, *9 Things You Simply Must Do*, 115.

to bend down and blow on the glowing embers to *fan* them back into a flame. Within seconds, the fire will be roaring again.[2]

In his second letter to young Timothy, the apostle Paul challenges his son in the faith to not let his fire die. Timothy is exhorted to "fan" the flame so that his gifts are fully activated, providing light and heat for the church. Paul was concerned that his protégé could become complacent, allowing his presence and contributions to become cold and lethargic. Timothy's situation is unique in the New Testament as he is the first known "second generation" Christian leader, having been introduced to the gospel by his faithful mother and grandmother.

You might be asking, "What am I good at? What gifts am I supposed to fan into flame?" There simply is not enough space on these pages to describe the gifts of a Peacemaker, but your gifts are vital for the health of the church and world.

Peacemakers are innately unselfish. Although they may work tirelessly, they don't like being in the spotlight. This focus on the *greater good* is over their own ego, which allows for their entire community to grow. As Beatrice Chestnut points out, "Nines may expend large amounts of energy working to further other people's projects or putting time into programs that improve the quality of life at work for the organization as a whole."[3]

> You are not an accident, and your natural gifts are part of a grand plan to create universal harmony.

Peacemakers intuitively grasp the needs of others and then focus on their success. Naturally devoid of most prejudice, they are nonjudgmental listeners who easily help people feel understood. They often become therapists, counselors, spiritual leaders, social workers, human resources managers, and fill other people-centric roles, because they can "sense what it is like to be inside the skin of the other person."[4]

---

2 "What Does It Mean to Fan into Flame the Gift of God?," Bibles for America Blog, July 20, 2018, https://blog.biblesforamerica.org/fan-into-flame-the-gift-of-god/.

3 Chestnut, *The 9 Types of Leadership*, 286-287.

4 Riso and Hudson, *The Wisdom*, 319.

Peacemakers are great team players. Some have said these super-friendly, agreeable, and steady type Nine co-workers are the easiest personality to work with. They don't become dramatic under pressure, but calmly stick to a routine. Rather than flying solo, they like to fly in formation and help the team go further, faster. "They take great pride in a group victory and can feel another player's triumph as their own,"[5] modeling inclusion, valuing diversity, and making decisions by consensus as much as possible. Thus, they often become the "project glue" that holds the team together.

Peacemakers frequently play the role of negotiator between two parties. Their ability to see all sides of an issue, defuse conflict, reconcile opposing views, seek compromise, and build consensus creates general harmony in what could otherwise be highly contentious work environments.

The Good News for Peacemakers is that you are not an accident, and your natural gifts are part of a grand plan to create universal harmony. You mirror Christ's mission of resolving discord between humanity and God. Jesus gave up His life on the cross "to redeem us from all lawlessness and to purify for himself a people for his own possession," but the verse doesn't stop there. The apostle Paul adds that the purified people are now, "zealous for good works."[6] A zealous follower of Jesus takes the Divine inspiration in all people and fans it into a flame of good works.

Remember, you didn't start the fire, so you can't put it out! Just as the disciples on the road to Emmaus exclaimed that their hearts were burning after being with Jesus,[7] so too have our hearts been ignited by the Holy Spirit and kept ablaze by walking with Jesus. Our only job is to keep fanning the flame!

---

5   Palmer, *The Enneagram in Love and Work*, 246.

6   Titus 2:14

7   Luke 24:32

➜ Pray

Father, I wouldn't be here without You or the friends and family who have invested in me. Thank You for giving me faithful people who have prayed for, taught, disciplined, modeled for, and led me. Help me to take inventory of the truths and gifts passed down to me with gratitude. Give me a heart that burns for You and a zeal for good works.

Day 15 Reflections:

Paul asked Timothy to take inventory of the spiritual deposit made by his mother and grandmother. What spiritual truths and gifts have been passed down to you from your family?

_____

_____

_____

Which of the strengths above have you been affirmed the most throughout your life?

_____

_____

_____

What's one thing you can do to ignite and develop your gifts?

_____

_____

_____

➜ Respond

Recruit three people to make a list of at least five things that they think you're good at.

Day 16:

Quiver of (Passive-Aggressive) Arrows

His speech was smooth as butter, yet war was in his heart; his words were softer than oil, yet they were drawn swords.

—Psalm 55:21

I'LL TAKE A WILD GUESS AND ASSUME you are not often referred to as *bossy, confrontational,* or *aggressive.* Healthy Peacemakers are known for being warmhearted, friendly, affectionate, polite, cheerful, hospitable, and sensitive. But, like all of us, Peacemakers have unhealthy sides that often come out when they experience heavy stress. Though Nines almost never outright attack, when backed into a corner they can become aggressive in a different way— aggressively *passive.*

While quietly withdrawing from conflict seems like the nicest thing to do, Riso and Hudson point out,

> Silence is a passive aggressive grenade thrown by insecure people that want war, but they don't want the accountability of starting it.
>
> —Shannon L. Alder[1]

---

1   "Learn To Communicate Quotes," Goodreads (Goodreads), accessed November 13, 2020, https://www.goodreads.com/quotes/tag/learn-to-communicate.

The irony is that their passivity and denials, their inattention to others, and their increasing disengagement from the environment are all negative forms of aggression—passive resistance—an aggressive withholding of themselves from reality. Nines are far more aggressive than they think they are.[2]

Enneagram teacher Ian Cron likens the passive-aggressive strategies of a Peacemaker to a quiver of arrows. In this invisible quiver are strategies such as avoidance, procrastination, stonewalling, tuning out, giving the silent treatment, or refusing to do tasks that you've been asked to do—more than once.[3]

King David's son Absalom had a few passive-aggressive arrows in his quiver, and when combined with natural charisma and a talent for manipulation, the result became deadly. After the prince murdered his brother Amnon, King David banished him from the kingdom. Absalom is later allowed to return, but is full of shame and hatred toward his father. Out

> Reconciliation with *our* enemies is no longer optional but becomes our daily ministry.

of anger and desperation, he asks David's commander, Joab, if he can set up a meeting between him and his father. When Joab refuses, Absalom redirects his anger and acts out for the attention he seeks by setting fire to Joab's fields.[4]

After finally securing a meeting with the king, the rebellious prince pretends to make peace, but secretly comes up with a shrewd plan to take over the kingdom from his father. He promises the citizens behind closed doors that if he is crowned, he will meet all of their needs in a way that David has not. Because of this scheme, "Absalom stole the hearts of the men of Israel."[5] At the right time, Absalom executes his secretly devised plan and sends his father packing in fear and shame from Jerusalem.

---

2 Riso and Hudson, *The Wisdom*, 343.

3 Cron and Stabile, *The Road Back to You*, 78.

4 2 Sam. 14:28-33

5 2 Sam. 15:6

Most commentators agree it was at this time David wrote Psalm 55, when he thought of what would be the last time he would see his son alive, "His speech was smooth as butter, yet war was in his heart; his words were softer than oil, yet they were drawn swords."[6] Absalom's actions demonstrate that passive-aggressive people can be even more dangerous than aggressive ones when their enemy doesn't know what's coming.

Remember that passive forms of resistance may infuriate others. Though open conflict is difficult, the surprise of a passive attack can often create more lasting harm for all involved. Plus, people are more perceptive than you think and can see right through the head nodding, smiling, and playing things off like they don't matter. Rather than undermining someone by telling them you'll do something when you really won't or spreading gossip and complaints about them to others, be upfront about your areas of disagreement.

Put simply: healthy people communicate. Overly passive people withhold themselves and say, "I don't matter," while aggressive people strike by saying, "You don't matter." Nines often take a different tactic, passive-aggressively saying in their heart, "You don't matter and I'm not going to let you know." Healthy people will say, "We both matter. Let's solve this issue so we can move forward together."

The Good News for Peacemakers is that God is not passive-aggressive. Pastor John Fooshee points out that Peacemakers will find the doctrine of *reconciliation* comforting:[7] "God shows his love for us in that while we were still sinners, Christ died for us. … while we were enemies we were reconciled to God."[8] Though God had every right to be angry with us, He sent Jesus to atone for our sins. Atonement means "at-one-ment." In other words, we are now "at one" with the Father because of Christ's work. This means as Christ followers, reconciliation with *our* enemies is no longer optional but becomes our daily ministry.[9]

---

6 Ps. 55:21

7 People Launching, "Gospel Enneagram," Gospel Enneagram, 2020, https://www.gospelenneagram.com.

8 Rom. 5:8-10

9 2 Cor. 5:19

→ Pray

Father, I'm thankful that I'll never be on the receiving end of any passive-aggressiveness from You. Thank You for turning me, an enemy, into Your friend forever. Help me to feel the weight of my calling to have a ministry of reconciliation. Charge me today to be someone who leans into tension and loves people by assuming the best about them and speaking the truth to their face rather than behind their back.

Day 16 Reflections:

How might your passivity look aggressive to others?

What passive-aggressive arrows do you pull out the most: avoidance, procrastination, stonewalling, tuning out, giving the silent treatment, not performing tasks that are clearly yours to do, and so on?

What does God do and say to reconcile with Adam and Eve in the garden? Can you think of any other biblical examples of reconciliation?

→ Respond

Passive-aggressive people often become frustrated because their unexpressed needs remain unmet. Practice making a detailed request with the fundamental Ws: Who would you like to make a request of? What do you want them to do exactly? Where and when should this request be fulfilled? Why is this important?

Day 17:

Wrestling With God

And Jacob was left alone. And a man wrestled with him until the breaking of

the day. When the man saw that he did not prevail against Jacob, he touched

his hip socket, and Jacob's hip was put out of joint as he wrestled with him. Then

he said, "Let me go, for the day has broken." But Jacob said, "I will not let you go

unless you bless me."

—Genesis 32:24-26

Wrestling with God
is a sign of intimacy.
You can't wrestle
with someone you're
far away from.

–Jon Acuff

ALTHOUGH I WAS A WRESTLER ALL FOUR years of high school, I am not naturally dominant. During my freshman year, I won two matches—but both were byes! However, by my senior year, I had 20 wins and was consistently improving. That year, I was one match away from making it to the state tournament, but as time wound down in the district finals, I found myself several points behind. Out of desperation, I threw a headlock and took my opponent to the ground, securing just enough points for the victory and a trip to state.

My showing in the next tournament was decent, but my coach believed I could have done more than compete—I could have excelled or medaled. Seeing potential, he took time during practice to wrestle me one-on-one, slapping me around, trying to do everything he could to cultivate that "killer instinct" in me. The only problem was, I was simply too nice. I wanted to win without hurting anyone!

One of the foundational tales of the Hebrew people is Jacob's wrestling match with God at the Jabbok River. The trickster has spent most of his life running from problems and staying one step ahead of the consequences. In fact, he's on *this* side of the Jabbok because his brother Esau (and his army) are on the other! As darkness falls, someone wrestles with Jacob as he lies near the water's edge, and there they struggle until the horizon begins to brighten.

> God delights in people who aren't afraid to strive and struggle.

Suddenly, God "touched" Jacob's hip socket, and his hip was thrown out of joint. Ouch! I'm glad my wrestling coach didn't go that far. In a surprising twist, Jacob (the runner, the "soft" one who fled from fights) has finally been pushed to the edge and developed a fighter mentality. God says, "Let me go" but Jacob replies, "I will not let you go until you bless me." The change of character has been achieved and Jacob is now ready to take the mantle of Patriarch: "Your name shall no longer be called Jacob, but Israel, for you have striven with God and with men, and have prevailed."[1]

From this story, it appears that God delights in people who aren't afraid to strive and struggle—*Israel* means "one who struggles with God." Though such an aggressive stance may feel counterintuitive to what we think God wants from us, Scripture constantly invites us to boldly assert ourselves—ask, seek, and knock.[2] Just look at David's psalms. A closer look will reveal a collection of "wrestling" prayers from someone who wasn't reprimanded for his doubts and questions

---

1   Gen. 32:28

2   Matt. 7:7-8

or his brutal honesty and boldness, but rather he was called a man after God's own heart.

Do you wrestle with God? Are you clear with Him on your questions and struggles—the parts of yourself and this world you want to see changed? Do you pour out your desperate needs, doubts, and anger? Do you remind Him of His character and promises and hold onto Him until you get His blessing?

Be assured God can take our doubts, anger, grief, and disappointment. Practice replacing your well-worded requests with raw emotion. (See Psalm 77.) God won't punish you or be disappointed. You have a Father who is more than willing to step into the ring with you; therefore, "let us then with confidence draw near to the throne of grace."[3]

The Good News for Peacemakers is that God wants to know you even when you are anxious or guarded. He knows why you resist being brutally honest and still invites you into openness with Him—and with yourself—for which He made you. You can let Him and others in because there's nothing left to fear. He's waiting to bless you today. Don't let God go until you receive His blessing!

→ Pray

Father, I admit that I hesitate to bring my full self to You when I pray. Give me the courage to pour out my heart with brutal honesty. I know You can take it. Thank You that people like Jacob and Jesus have shown me what it is to faithfully struggle with You. I commit myself to strive for Your blessing everyday by anchoring my confidence in Your unchanging character.

---

3 Heb. 4:16

Day 17 Reflections:

What are you afraid to say to God?

What if you didn't measure the success of your prayer life by how often you pray or how kind you are but by how honest you are?

After his wrestling match with God, Jacob—now Israel—walks away with a limp. What lessons have you learned in life that may have left you wounded but more ready to serve?

→ Respond

Read Psalm 77 and observe how vulnerable and honest Asaph is with the Lord. After meditating on the Psalm, try offering a prayer to the Lord with the same level of honesty.

Day 18:

Living Through Others

The woman said to him, "Sir, give me this water, so that I will not be thirsty or

have to come here to draw water." Jesus said to her, "Go, call your husband, and

come here." The woman answered him, "I have no husband." Jesus said to her,

"You are right in saying, 'I have no husband'; for you have had five husbands,

and the one you now have is not your husband. What you have said is true."

—John 4:15-18

ANDRE AGASSI, ONE OF THE GREATEST TENNIS players of all time, said, "I play tennis for a living even though I hate tennis, hate it with a dark and secret passion and always have." In his autobiography, *Open*, he spoke of a father who was unable to "tell the difference between loving me and loving tennis."[2]

> If you live for people's acceptance you will die from their rejection.
>
> —Lecrae[1]

What drove Agassi to succeed was not a love for tennis but a desire to win the love of his hard-to-please father. Much like the tennis

---

1   Lecrae. Twitter Post. August 14, 2012, 8:37 AM. https://twitter.com/lecrae/status/235369514517286912.

2   Agassi, *Open*, 202.

legend, Peacemakers will do almost anything to secure the sense of acceptance they crave. This is why Peacemakers can easily fall into traditional roles that are not self-chosen but *assigned* by someone else or even by the broader culture—homemaker, breadwinner, doctor, lawyer, athlete, and so on.[3]

The Peacemaker's superpower is *empathy*: the ability to see and experience the world through someone else's eyes. But, as with all strengths, it becomes a weakness when it becomes *merging*. When we merge, we don't merely experience the world from someone else's view, we lose ourselves completely in their lives. As artist Ryan O'Neal from Sleeping At Last sings, "It looks like empathy, to understand all sides, but I'm just trying to find myself through someone else's eyes."[4]

> Peacemakers can easily fall into traditional roles that are not self-chosen but assigned by someone else.

One Peacemaker perfectly describes this tension in Marilyn Vancil's book *Self to Lose Self to Find*:

> "This is my biggest struggle. I can be on my own road and the next thing I know I'm on someone else's road without even being aware of how I got swept away. Sometimes I feel like I'm bouncing around—doing what I'm expected to do—but not necessarily living how I want to live. I'm learning to check in with myself more. … I need to ask if I am giving up too much of myself for the priorities of someone else."[5]

Whereas some Enneagram types live *for* others, Peacemakers live *through* others. The strongest desire is not finding a sense of worth through vicarious participation in others' experiences, whether they be a romantic relationship, children, politics, religion, athletics, career, addiction, or other experiences. Once merged with these experiences, it can be nearly impossible to separate. Due to the Peacemakers' natural apathy, one who is merged will likely remain so unless

---

3   Riso and Hudson, *The Wisdom*, 354.

4   Ryan O'Neal, "Sleeping At Last," Sleeping At Last, 2016, http://sleepingatlast.com.

5   Vancil, *Self to Lose Self to Find*, 134.

influenced by an outside force, such as a relationship break-up, getting fired, or other life-altering events.

In John's Gospel, we meet a person who has come to be simply known as "the woman at the well." Jesus breaks many cultural norms by speaking privately with this Samaritan woman and surprises her with His knowledge of her life, particularly her relational history. Though her community undoubtedly knew this history, an outsider had no way of knowing. Jesus' insight cuts to the heart of her experience. She had already been with five husbands and is now living—unmarried—with a sixth man.

We are not told why she has been married so many times, but Jesus seems not to care. Life for an unmarried woman—particularly a divorcée or widow—has always been difficult, especially in this context. However, Jesus does not seek to judge, but is filled with acceptance and love. Throughout their conversation, He invites her into a deeper relationship than she has ever known.

Through Jesus' pointing out of her constant merging, this beloved woman comes to see her inner thirst. Ernest Becker calls this "apocalyptic romance," the idea that we can "look to sex and romance to give us the transcendence and sense of meaning [and security] we used to get from faith in God."[6] Jesus offers her (and us) another way.

The Good News for Peacemakers is that Jesus promises those who merge with Him will never go thirsty. We will be brought into a full, thriving relationship with the Father, with whom we can always be our true selves. We can stop basing our self-esteem on the people and groups we are associated with, and instead, find our identity in God. Then and only then will our self-worth not be swept away when the relationship fails, our kids leave the house, or we have a community "fall out." When our identity is merged with something greater than us, rather than losing ourselves, we become more of who we were meant to be.

---

6   Keller, Timothy. *Counterfeit Gods: The Empty Promises of Money, Sex, and Power, and the Only Hope That Matters* (United States: Penguin Publishing Group, 2011), 28.

→ Pray

Father, help me to return to the fountain of living water. Forgive me for carving out cisterns that are broken and cannot hold any water. Enable me to let go of everything this world has to offer so that I may cling to You. My only hope in life and death is that I am united to You. For from You and through You and to You are all things. To You be glory forever.[7]

Day 18 Reflections:

In what ways do you feel smarter, stronger, safer, and more secure when you merge with a person or a group? Are you more likely to find your identity in an individual or a group?

How do you know if you are making a decision because the Spirit of Truth put an idea in your heart or someone else told you to?

What expectations do the people in your life have of you? What would happen if you became convinced that pleasing God meant going in a different direction?

→ Respond

Take a day for solitude. Silence the voices around you, and write out what you sense God calling you to do.

7 Rom. 11:36

Day 19:

Becoming Your Own Person

Rather, speaking the truth in love, we are to grow up in every way into him who is the head, into Christ, from whom the whole body, joined and held together by every joint with which it is equipped, when each part is working properly, makes the body grow so that it builds itself up in love.

—Ephesians 4:15-16

WHEN YOU WALK INTO SOMEONE'S HOME AND notice a portrait hanging on the wall, your eyes are most likely drawn to the image rather than the frame. A good frame supports and enhances what lies within. A Peacemaker can feel like the "frame" of their own life, as if no one really sees *them*, but instead notices everyone and everything they support through their (largely unnoticed) efforts. Without realizing it, they even forget to look at themselves as their

> I check my vital signs.
> choked up, I realize
> I've been less than half myself
> for more than half my life.
>
> –Sleeping At Last, "Nine"[1]

---

1   Ryan O'Neal, "Sleeping At Last," Sleeping At Last, 2016, http://sleepingatlast.com.

attention is drawn to the person or group of people in the frame with whom they have merged.[2]

A frame is a fitting description for the Peacemaker because of their ability to encapsulate every type. As Ian Cron explains:

> "Nines can embody the idealism of Ones, the kindness of Twos, the attractiveness of Threes, the creativity of Fours, the intellectual horsepower of Fives, the loyalty of Sixes, the optimism and adventurousness of Sevens, and the strength of Eights. Unfortunately, from this privileged position Nines tend to see the world from the viewpoint of every number but their own."[3]

Having the ability to see the world through everyone else's eyes can lead you to *erase* yourself entirely—causing you to depend on others' ideas, feelings, agendas, and positions. Therefore, the path of growth is toward autonomy.

The church has often downplayed the need for autonomy: you won't hear very many positive sermons on its value. Almost every resource on the subject focuses on the negative aspects of separating ourselves from the bonds of community.

Though it's absolutely true that we *do* need to depend on God and others, the apostle Paul's illustration of the church as a body demonstrates that each part must depend on the others to fulfill its own unique role. The ear cannot depend on the eye to do the job of hearing nor can the eye depend on the ear to do its seeing. Furthermore, Paul adds that the church is built up "when each part is working properly."[4] In other words, *healthy interdependence* depends upon *healthy independence*.

> Having the ability to see the world through everyone else's eyes can lead you to erase yourself entirely.

---

2 Riso and Hudson, *The Wisdom*, 324.

3 Cron and Stabile, *The Road*, 69.

4 Eph. 4:16

Henry Cloud warns that people who are overly dependent tend to be less successful than their co-workers, often passively relying on others to do the work.[5] Another implication for the workplace is that seeing things from every perspective can lead to the belief that "all sides are equal when they aren't."[6] Leadership often requires making difficult decisions. Enneagram teacher Helen Palmer notes that always pushing for a consensus could just be a strategy to protect ourselves from blame if the results go sideways.

When it comes to relationships, Peacemakers who are overly merged with family or friends may find their world coming apart when those people fall into addictions or serious crises.[7] In addition, Peacemakers may find it hard to break ties with the wrong people and continue unhealthy relationships for years. This not only extends possible trauma, but also prevents new, healthy relationships from forming.[8] Because Peacemakers desire to attach themselves to stronger, aggressive, more energetic people to provide "juice" for their lives, things can backfire when others take advantage of them and they are left feeling empty.[9]

The Good News for Peacemakers is that their natural empathic impulses are a reflection of the Trinity. The church has long taught the mystery that God is *one*, yet exists as three distinct Persons. The Father, Son, and Holy Spirit are merged together in a symbiotic relationship, all while retaining unique personalities and roles. The Trinity is a perfect illustration to satisfy the soul of a Peacemaker, but such a healthy relational dynamic requires health on all sides. C. S. Lewis echoes the church fathers when speaking of God's interdependence as "a dynamic, pulsating activity, a life, almost a kind of drama ... a kind of dance."[10]

As Trinitarian image bearers, you are invited into the dance. To show up with your full, autonomously interdependent self, continuing to learn who God has made you to be. Don't let anyone else force you down their path; instead, walk in the footsteps of God.

---

5   Cloud, *9 Things You Simply Must Do*, 100.

6   Wagner, *Nine Lenses.*

7   Riso and Hudson, *The Wisdom*, 328.

8   Palmer, *The Enneagram in Love and Work*, 235-236.

9   Riso and Hudson, *The Wisdom*, 328.

10   C. S. Lewis, *Mere Christianity* (1952; Harper Collins: 2001) 174-176.

→ **Pray**

Father, You created me to depend on You and no one else. Give me a resurgence of confidence through the Holy Spirit not to depend on anyone else to do the work You've prepared for me. Forgive me for thinking that I don't have what it takes to fulfill my purpose. Remind me that I can do all things through Christ who strengthens me.

Day 19 Reflections:

When has codependency shown up in your past?

_____

_____

_____

What qualities do you tend to notice first in others? How do these fulfill what you believe you lack?

_____

_____

_____

Where are your relationship expectations coming from?

_____

_____

_____

→ **Respond**

Reflecting on the examples given in the last paragraph of today's devotion, name one step you can take to move toward greater autonomy.

Day 20:

Decide Rather Than Slide

I will instruct you and teach you in the way you should go; I will counsel you

with my eye upon you.

—Psalm 32:8

WHY CAN IT BE SO DIFFICULT TO decide to break off a long-term relationship? Why are even simple changes—such as switching credit cards, internet providers, or moving from Apple to Google products—difficult for many people? In behavioral economics, this apathy is called *consumer lock-in*, which describes the decreased likelihood to search for or change to another option once people have invested in something because the switching costs are too high.

> You don't need more time. You just need to decide.
>
> –Seth Godin[1]

In other words, if you merge with a person, brand, or group long enough, it may become too difficult for you to leave when appropriate or even necessary. So, you will *slide* rather than *decide*. Sliding is a real struggle for Peacemakers; the desire to be firm and

---

1   2011 February 9, "You Don't Need More Time," Seth's Blog, February 9, 2011, https://seths.blog/2011/02/you-dont-need-more-time/.

conclusive is there, but it's just too easy to slide into analysis paralysis and allow others to make decisions for us.

Peacemakers often make decisions by a process of elimination. As Helen Palmer notes, "They may not know what they want, but they know what they don't want when they're uncomfortable. … 'Not that, not that' is a path toward clarifying real goals, without having to know exactly where you're headed."[2]

This difficulty has many potential sources. You may be afraid your decision will pin you down or be afraid of others' reactions, which can create the unwillingness to choose: "Is it worth

> Not deciding *is* a decision.

it to defend my position and create a conflict here?" If you feel powerless, then you may think, "I really don't have a say in this anyway." Additionally, a lack of certainty or ability to discern the differences in a debate may keep you on the fence until everyone else comes to a consensus that you can join.

But not deciding *is* a decision.

The challenge for a Peacemaker is to allow others to see your "drafts" rather than your "final edit." As Palmer points out:

> "Mediators inadvertently create [conflict] by withholding information during the decision-making phase. Nine leaders are famous for not filling people in while they ponder, and for delivering the final decision without explanation or comment. Bad news may seem to come out of the blue without warning. It may seem less conflictual to send pink slips in the mail without comment rather than to face a series of difficult meetings to explain why those slips are necessary."[3]

Scripture teaches Peacemakers how to add decisiveness to their gift of patience. Before the Israelites crossed the Jordan into the promised land, the long-suffering Moses confronted his backsliding people to make a decisive choice: "I call heaven and earth to witness against you today, that I have set before you life and death,

---

2 Palmer, *The Enneagram in Love and Work*, 237-238.

3 Ibid, 243.

blessing and curse. Therefore choose … ."[4] Similarly, once they had conquered most of the region, Moses' successor, Joshua, reiterated the call: "Choose this day whom you will serve, whether the gods your fathers served in the region beyond the River, or the gods of the Amorites … ."[5] Much later in the Israelites' story, the prophet Elijah offered the same choice: " 'How long will you go limping between two different opinions? If the Lord is God, follow him; but if Baal, then follow him.' And the people did not answer him a word."[6]

The Good News for Peacemakers is that God promises to guide and empower our decision-making."[7] We have been given the "mind of Christ"[8] so that we might *think* rightly, and with the Spirit of Christ, so that we may *do* rightly. God also gave us bodies intended to be deeply connected to both our mind and spirit. Drew Moser points out that Peacemakers are in the "gut" triad, which means they have a high "GQ," or gut intelligence. This refers to the ability to intuitively know something to be true even before all the facts have been gathered. Moser says, "By engaging our bodies in activity, we open up our intelligence viscerally, utilizing sensations and instincts."[9] Because Peacemakers have a propensity to fall asleep and become numb to these sensations, you must remember to listen to your whole self when seeking discernment, bringing all the God-given wisdom you have into every decision.

→ Pray

Father, grant me the serenity to accept the things I cannot change, the courage to change the things I can, and the wisdom to know the difference.

---

4   Deut. 30:19-20

5   Josh. 24:15

6   1 Kings 18:21

7   Ps. 32:8

8   1 Cor. 2:16

9   Moser, Drew. *The Enneagram of Discernment: The Way of Vocation, Wisdom, and Practice* (Beaver Falls, PA: Falls City Press, 2020), 78.

Day 20 Reflections:

When has indecisiveness revealed itself in your life?

What do you think kept Jesus from being indecisive? Read and reflect on Jesus' understanding of His call in Luke 9:51.

What specific fears stop you from making a decision in the moment?

How would decision-making become easier if you knew you could change your mind later without penalty and receive unlimited forgiveness for every bad decision? How can you begin to separate yourself from the paralyzing fear of wrong choices?

→ Respond

Think about a decision that must be made soon. Before you observe how you think or feel about it, explain what your gut is telling you to do.

Day 21:

Peacemaking Over Peacefaking

For in him all the fullness of God was pleased to dwell, and through him to reconcile to himself all things, whether on earth or in heaven, making peace by the blood of his cross.

—Colossians 1:19-20

> Making other people happy isn't a good gauge for whether I'm acting as a Peacemaker.
>
> –Alison L. Bradley[1]

PEACEMAKERS ARE ESPECIALLY SUITED TO TAKE ON the "ministry of reconciliation."[2] Intuitively understanding why others are upset, Peacemakers listen thoroughly to complaints, identify differences, find common ground, and have the ability to "pour oil on troubled waters."[3] However, when "keep calm" becomes your motto for everything, *peacemaking*

---

1   Alison L. Bradley (@9ish_andiknowit), "We talked about listening to our emotions and time alone to listen to ourselves this week, but it can be hard to believe that these are the path to peace or loving others best." *Instagram*, June 12, 2020. Accessed November 15, 2020. https://www.instagram.com/p/CBV3tH9JVj0/.

2   2 Cor. 5:18

3   Riso and Hudson, *The Wisdom*, 351.

becomes *peacefaking*. Remember, peace is not found in the absence of conflict but in the active pursuit of creating wholeness.

The popular "Keep calm and carry on" posters produced in Britain at the onset of World War II are found all over the world, with a variety of motivational and humorous changes. In some extreme seasons, all we can do is resolve our will and remain calm through the storm. Ultimately, if we do not actively take steps to change the circumstances, even the most stoic and calm will crack. The British people were able to keep calm because they trusted their leaders to work night and day to bring real peace.

Even Abraham struggled throughout his life with settling for false peace. Ironically, he also shows us the first "hard bargain" between humanity and God. When confronted by Sodom's wickedness, the typically unassertive patriarch steps up to actively intercede.

With stunning forthrightness, he demands of God, "Will you indeed sweep away the righteous with the wicked? Suppose there are fifty righteous within the city. Will you then sweep away the place and not spare it for the fifty righteous who are in it? Far be it from you to do such a thing, to put the righteous to death with the wicked, so that the righteous fare as the wicked! Far be that from you! Shall not the Judge of all the earth do what is just?"[4]

> When "keep calm" becomes your motto for everything, *peacemaking* becomes *peacefaking.*

Because of Abraham's boldness, God agrees to save the city if 50 righteous people are found. But the number is not the point, as both parties know. Rather, God is drawing out Abraham's care and confidence until he is pressing God to save the city for 10 people. Although that city was not able to be saved, this story is an example of Peacemakers' ability to bring wholeness to the world if they resist the urge to people-please and assert themselves instead.

---

4   Gen. 18:23-25

Abraham was *peacemaking* rather than *peacefaking*. What's the difference? Ken Sande, in his book *The Peacemaker: A Biblical Guide to Resolving Personal Conflict* says that Peace*fakers* deny conflict or flee when they fear that relationships will be damaged.

In contrast, the work of Peace*making* involves strategies of active involvement: *negotiation, mediation,* and *intervention.*[5] Negotiation is taking the initiative to contact the other person to sit down and discuss how each party could find their legitimate needs met.[6] Mediation is taking the initiative to find outside "referees" (or to take on this role) to listen to each party and explore helpful solutions. Lastly, intervention is taking the initiative to hold someone accountable to their laws, values, and faith.

The common denominators in these Peacemaking strategies are *leaning in* and *taking the initiative.* Our peacefaking "escape" strategies only serve to erode the foundation of reconciliation and short-circuit the process of true restoration.

The Good News for Peacemakers is that Jesus took the initiative to reconcile humanity to God by "making peace by the blood of the cross."[7] Peacemaking comes at a cost. Our Great High Priest, the One whom Abraham pointed to, continues to intercede on our behalf—reminding us of the restoration He achieved.[8] Pastor John Fooshee says a Peacemaker is one who fights *from* peace rather than *for* peace.[9] When we are internally stable and sure of our peace with the Divine, we are able to offer that peace to the world.

The story of Abraham and Sodom begs the question: Would God have saved the city for *one* righteous person? The cross gives us a resounding "Yes!" God the Father was pleased to save every person of every city from every generation because of the righteousness of His one and only Son. This is the message and hope that sends us into the world as agents of reconciliation.

---

5   *Merge Premarital Class* (Dallas: Watermark Community Church, 2010), 28.

6   Phil. 2:4

7   Col. 1:19-20

8   Rom. 8:34

9   People Launching, "Gospel Enneagram," Gospel Enneagram, 2020, https://www.gospelenneagram.com.

→ **Pray**

Father, along with St. Francis, my prayer is this: "Make me an instrument of your peace. Where there is hatred, let me sow love." Thank You for sending Your Son, the ultimate Peacemaker, to reconcile the world to Yourself. Thank You for not counting our trespasses against us. Help me to fully embrace the calling You've given me to be a minister of reconciliation.[10]

Day 21 Reflections:

How have you played the role of peacemaker well in your family, work, church, or city?

Is the goal of your peacemaking efforts to pursue "calmness" or "wholeness?"

How did Jesus demonstrate the difference between peacefaking (denial and flight) and peacemaking (negotiation, mediation, and intervention)?

→ **Respond**

Choose one of these strategies to execute right now. Set up a time to negotiate meeting your needs, ask an outside "referee" to mediate a personal or work conflict, or initiate an intervention for someone you love who is in trouble or causing trouble.

10   2 Cor. 5:17-19

Day 22:
Becoming Unstoppable

Go to the ant, O sluggard; consider her ways, and be wise. Without having any

chief, officer, or ruler, she prepares her bread in summer and gathers her food

in harvest. How long will you lie there, O sluggard? When will you arise from

your sleep? A little sleep, a little slumber, a little folding of the hands to rest, and

poverty will come upon you like a robber, and want like an armed man.

—Proverbs 6:6-11

WHAT DO YOU WANT TO ACCOMPLISH, BUT don't feel like you have the time nor energy to start? The most difficult aspect of any project—especially for Nines—is often beginning. Jim Collins, in his bestselling book *Good to Great*, describes six things that separate good companies from great ones. One of his distinctions is called *The Flywheel Effect*:

> Big wins are usually a collection of very small steps.
>
> –Henry Cloud[1]

Picture a huge, heavy flywheel—a massive metal disk mounted horizontally on an axle, about 30 feet in diameter, 2 feet thick, and weighing about 5,000 pounds. Now

---

1 Cloud, *9 Things You Simply Must Do*, 84.

imagine that your task is to get the flywheel rotating on the axle as fast and long as possible. Pushing with great effort, you get the flywheel to inch forward, moving almost imperceptibly at first. You keep pushing and, after two or three hours of persistent effort, you get the flywheel to complete one entire turn. You keep pushing, and the flywheel begins to move a bit faster, and with continued great effort, you move it around a second rotation. … Then, at some point— breakthrough! The momentum of the thing kicks in in your favor, hurling the flywheel forward, turn after turn … whoosh! … its own heavy weight working for you. You're pushing no harder than during the first rotation, but the flywheel goes faster and faster.[2]

Collins uses this metaphor to point out that great companies' success comes from a series of small efforts rather than one "magic push." An ancient version of the flywheel metaphor is the hardworking ant found in Proverbs. Do you want to finish a dissertation, write a book, start a ministry, or get that degree? Just look down and "consider the ant," as Scripture suggests.[3] The ant works tirelessly, and through slow, small movements, stores up what it needs to last through the winter. If an ant can do it, can't you?

Peacemakers are constantly fighting low energy and wandering attention. Those first few pushes of the flywheel are incredibly difficult. It's much easier to jump on someone else's flywheel and run off of their momentum. But don't give up!

> Success comes from a series of small efforts rather than one "magic push."

Helen Palmer offers some encouragement: "The principle of inertia states that a physical body at rest tends to stay at rest, and a body in motion tends to stay in motion. Nines say that they need a jump start to get rolling, and that once they get into gear they're unstoppable."[4] Likely, you have noticed this about yourself: When you have forced yourself to keep going on something, you eventually find that you have the strength to finish. Like the hard working ant, remaining cool,

---

2   "The Flywheel Effect," Jim Collins - Concepts - The Flywheel Effect, accessed November 16, 2020, https://www.jimcollins.com/concepts/the-flywheel.html.

3   Proverbs 6:6-8

4   Palmer, *The Enneagram in Love and Work*, 231-232.

calm, steady, and steadfast—without a desire for attention—you will outlast the competition.

The Good News for Peacemakers is that God provides the power for us to "run with endurance the race that is set before us"[5] by fixing our eyes on Jesus who *endured* on our behalf. Furthermore, Paul tells the Galatian church, "And let us not grow weary of doing good, for in due season we will reap, if we do not give up."[6] Remember, God measures success by our *faithfulness,* not results. We execute the small, daily steps of planting and watering, but in the end we will say, "God ... gives the growth."[7]

→ Pray

Father, forgetting what lies behind and straining forward to what lies ahead, I will press on toward the goal of fulfilling my calling in Christ Jesus. Forgive me for too often resorting to slumber when I should be doing the work to which You've called me. I receive Your forgiveness today and ask that You help me to rise and run my race with endurance.

---

5   Heb. 12:1-2

6   Gal. 6:9

7   1 Cor. 3:5-7

Day 22 Reflections:

Why do fast-tracks to success fall short of biblical wisdom?

When have you seen the flywheel effect playing out in your life? What lessons can you learn from your past successes?

Who can you recruit to help you "push" through the initial resistance of beginning a project?

→ Respond

Big successes start with small steps. Start a 10-minute daily workout. Set a goal to pay off a set amount of debt this month. Make a call to a counselor. Devote 10 minutes toward cleaning a different room each day this week. Moving one grain of sand every day gets the flywheel going.

Day 23:

Getting Distracted

[Jesus] said, "Follow me." But he said, "Lord, let me first go and bury my father."

And Jesus said to him, "Leave the dead to bury their own dead. But as for you,

go and proclaim the kingdom of God." Yet another said, "I will follow you, Lord,

but let me first say farewell to those at my home." Jesus said to him, "No one

who puts his hand to the plow and looks back is fit for the kingdom of God."

—Luke 9:59-62

HAVE YOU EVER SET OUT TO ACCOMPLISH a task and an hour later found yourself making progress on something entirely different? Dr. Jerome Wagner explains that Nines "distract themselves by cleaning out their desk drawers, getting a cup of coffee, suddenly remembering a friend they were going to call, lying down for a minute to take a nap, and so forth. After several hours have gone by, they remember what they were supposed to do, figure it's too late to do it now, and put it off till tomorrow."[2]

> If you don't prioritize your life, someone else will.
>
> —Greg McKeown[1]

---

1   Greg McKeown, "If You Don't Prioritize Your Life, Someone Else Will," *Harvard Business Review*, July 23, 2014, https://hbr.org/2012/06/how-to-say-no-to-a-controlling.

2   Wagner, *Nine Lenses on the World*.

While this daily adventure of twists and turns may sound fun, this "pinball machine lifestyle" of bouncing from one task to the next or one person to the next will eventually take all your change. The Apostle Paul tells Timothy to instruct the church to resist the busybody syndrome.[3] Busybodies, while always having something to do, are rarely occupied with the things they should (and actually want) to be doing.

Just as Peacemakers sometimes feel as if all opinions are of equal value and worth, they also find it hard to prioritize equally pressing concerns, which often leads to ignoring *all* concerns and spending time on activities requiring less thought or care. Today's passage highlights the tension of desiring to prioritize Jesus in the midst of everyday life. One man asks to stay and "bury [his] father" which sounds reasonable, but that phrase doesn't mean his father is already dead. Rather, his request is to remain with his aging father until he passes, which could delay following Jesus indefinitely. Jesus challenges the man to take the step that is necessary for today's needs, rather than using worries for the future as an excuse for inactivity.

> You don't have to fret over knowing the next 10 steps. You just have to know the next best thing.

Prioritizing is simply the act of designating value to the tasks at hand and then completing them in their order of importance. Identifying what your "big rocks" are (as the old illustration goes) and putting them in the jar first. Getting distracted causes us to shuffle that order, which often results in busywork filling up the jar quickly, leaving no room for the things we know are most important. So, how do we keep things in the right order?

Fundamentally, the Christian life is about loving God and others. One of the most foundational ways we love God is *through* loving our neighbors. Our big rocks, or our primary tasks, are to reimagine the people in our lives as objects of love. True, Christlike productivity means putting people first. With loving God and others at the top of God's scorecard, we can then ask: What's the next best thing?[4]

---

3 1 Tim. 5:13

4 For more help in the area of productivity read *What's Best Next* by Matthew Perman.

The core principle of productivity is this: know what's most important and put it first. To do this, you can't just rearrange all the urgent needs that arise in the whirlwind of life on sticky notes. You must control your schedule before your schedule controls you. As productivity guru Stephen Covey says, "The key is not to prioritize what's on your schedule, but to schedule your priorities."[5]

You can see the struggle here, right? Our primary task is loving God by actively loving people, but that doesn't necessarily mean we are required to be at everyone's beck and call. Some people's needs must be placed above others'. If you are a son, daughter, student, spouse, or employee, then part of it what it means to "love others" is to prioritize what *they* have asked of you. Make sure you don't get distracted from fulfilling your responsibilities to them. Ask them this week: What's the most important thing you'd like me to do this week?

The Good News for Peacemakers is that God "will instruct you and teach you in the way you should go."[6] You don't have to be a time management guru to be productive. If you carve out time to sit in the presence of God this week, you only have to wait for Him to say, "Follow me." Through the Spirit, we are guided to truth and toward our purpose of seeing Christ in all people and loving Him through them. You don't have to fret over knowing the next 10 steps. You just have to know the next best thing.

→ Pray

Father, I get distracted by many things. It's hard to stay focused on what's most important. But when I look at Your Son, Jesus, I see a Man with focus. He had to tell people no often to stay on task and show love to many. He filtered everything through loving You and loving people. Give me that same focus. Tell me what I am to do next and who I am to love. I'm listening.

---

5   Stephen R. Covey, *7 Habits of Highly Effective People* (Switzerland: Free Press, 2004), 161.

6   Ps. 32:8

Day 23 Reflections:

How has procrastination affected your life and relationships?

_____

_____

_____

_____

What do other people keep asking you to do but you keep avoiding?

_____

_____

_____

_____

When can you block out an hour to sit with Jesus and schedule your priorities this week?

_____

_____

_____

_____

➔ Respond

Practice the "hardest-first" technique. Create a to-do list for today, and then reorder the list putting the "hardest" tasks first. Spending your energy on resolving these things quicker will eliminate the prolonged anxiety caused by avoiding.[7]

---

7   Moser, _The Enneagram of Discernment,_ 148.

Day 24:

Powerful Productivity

"All things are lawful," but not all things are helpful. "All things are lawful," but

not all things build up.

—1 Corinthians 10:23

ARE THERE AREAS OF YOUR LIFE OR work that feel beyond your control, as though that conversation will never occur, or that project will never get done. Despite their calm, retiring demeanor, Peacemakers can be powerful leaders, but they are often left feeling scattered and absentminded. They may "stare at the clock but not see the time," or may seem more like a "woolgatherer," picking up tidbits of information here and there to ponder or discuss.[2]

> Aimless, unproductive Christians contradict the creative, purposeful, powerful, merciful God we love.
>
> –John Piper[1]

Ian Cron points out that this lack of focus sometimes leads to a meandering style of conversing. Listening to Nines talk about their day can easily become an "epic saga" with a "drawn-out story containing more

---

1   John Piper, *Don't Waste Your Life (Group Study Edition)* (Wheaton, IL: Crossway, 2007), 48.

2   Riso and Hudson, *Personality Types,* 357-358.

details and detours than you ever thought possible."[3] For Peacemakers, "rabbit trails" are both a way of relating and a way of delaying.

If you learn how to constrain your positive energy rather than allowing it to diffuse, your impact can greatly expand. The Colorado River is a powerful force precisely because the walls of the Grand Canyon constrain it. The narrowness of the river gives it more power and the canyon itself pays tribute to that power over the millennia. However, as the river heads south toward the desert in Arizona, it becomes stagnant and swamp-like. As it spreads out, it loses vitality.

Freedom is good but it can become an enemy of focus. Paul addresses those in the Corinthian church who were carrying a "I have the right to do anything" mindset. Their Christian liberty became an excuse to eat meat offered to idols in front of their brothers and sisters—fellow believers whose consciences wouldn't allow them to do the same. Paul reminded them that while it was lawful for them to eat this food biblically, it wasn't helpful to their relationships.

> Productivity is not about getting more things done, but accomplishing the *right* things.

You can apply this same principal to time management. There are many things we are "free" to do that may be permissible, but not productive. Instead of measuring productivity by how well we fill up our day, we should measure results. Productivity is not about getting more things done, but accomplishing the *right* things.

Maria Goff advises, "Figure out what you're good at and what you're not so good at. Keep it simple. Do more of what you're good at and less of everything else."[4] What would you do if you had all the time and money in the world or could only do one thing for the next five years? Once you've *defined* the work, then you can begin to reduce your workload and free yourself to do what you've been called to do.

---

3   Cron and Stabile, *The Road Back to You*, 71.

4   Maria Goff, *Love Lives Here* (Nashville: B&H Publishing Group, 2017), 134.

Tim Challies, author of *Do More Better: A Practical Guide to Productivity*, shares three simple things you can do with your tasks: *Drop, Delegate, or Do.*[5]

Drop the things that are taking up energy, but not serving a clear purpose. Have the courage to say *no* more. You may also need to defer tasks that aren't urgent. Exercising the self-control to flag those not-so-important emails for later may be the best thing you do today.

Delegate. You determine which things only you can do (and no one else) and delegate the rest. Ask yourself, "Is there someone else who could do this better?"

Do what needs to be done without procrastinating. If you need to, create some incentives for yourself as motivation to get it done!

The Good News for Peacemakers is that we have the Spirit of Jesus to help us discern the path of most effectiveness. He's shared the Holy Spirit, who will produce the self-control you need to do less and do it better. We may not be able to see the current of the river of God's will, but it is not difficult to feel when we are swimming with or against it. As Frederick Buechner says, "The place God calls you to is the place where your deep gladness and the world's deep hunger meet."[6]

→ Pray

Father, You are the God of miracles. I'm in awe of how You display Your power. I admit that I've been careless and unfocused at times with the tools You've given me. I need Your divine power to harness the energy You've given me. Please sharpen my axe and help me wield it for Your plans and purposes.

---

5   Tim Challies, *Do More Better: A Practical Guide to Productivity* (United States: Cruciform Press, 2015), 41.

6   Frederick Buechner, *Wishful Thinking* (London, Mowbray, 1994), 119.

Day 24 Reflections:

What things do you love and do better than others?

_____

_____

_____

_____

Thinking about your mission, what do you need to do more of? What do you need to drop?

_____

_____

_____

_____

What things can you delegate right now?

_____

_____

_____

_____

➜ Respond

Read a good book on productivity.

Day 25:

Work Out Your Salvation

Therefore, my beloved, as you have always obeyed, so now, not only as in my presence but much more in my absence, work out your own salvation with fear and trembling, for it is God who works in you, both to will and to work for his good pleasure.

—Philippians 2:12-13

MY WIFE, LINDSEY, AND I TRY TO take a marriage vacation to a new city every year. One of our favorite places we've visited is San Francisco. After walking the city for a week, we hopped in our rental car and traveled north to Muir Woods, a large redwood forest where some of the trees reach 250 feet high and 30 feet in diameter! I had seen images of these magnificent giants of nature before, but standing next to them was an entirely different experience.

> Grace is not opposed to effort, it is opposed to earning.
>
> –Dallas Willard[1]

Walking through the forest, it was hard for us to comprehend that some of these were mere sprouting seeds when Jesus walked the earth 2,000 years ago. How does

---

1   Dallas Willard, *The Great Omission: Reclaiming Jesus's Essential Teachings on Discipleship* (United Kingdom: Harper-Collins, 2006), 61.

something so big come from something so small, and how does it survive so long? Every seed, though it's not immediately apparent, has the imprint of something much bigger within it.

The same is true of *you*. God has imprinted the Divine image on your soul, and though your faith may begin smaller than a redwood seed, it has the potential to grow into something truly magnificent. You were not created to be a small house plant, but a giant redwood that can weather endless storms.

> Decide how you want to become more like Jesus and start becoming that person right now.

Jesus came into the world because He saw that the human forest was on fire. The prophet Isaiah said that a Messiah would come to save His people, to replant the forest under a new covenant of growth so that "they may be called oaks of righteousness."[2] Like a seed, if we go into the ground and die[3] to our old self, we will be renewed after the image of our Creator.[4] Our path of salvation includes "letting go" of our disordered desires and placing ourselves in the trustworthy hands of our Master Gardener. Though you have been sown perishable, Jesus offers to raise you imperishable.[5] The glorious reward of trusting in Jesus is eternal life.

However, this step is just the beginning. Though we don't work *for* our salvation, we must work *out* our salvation. This statement might sound a little confusing, so let me explain. Working *for* our salvation is the path of religion—obeying God in order to win His approval and blessing through a sanctioned set of beliefs, words, and actions. The gospel is translated "good news" precisely because everything we receive from God is an undeserved gift—including our eternal salvation. We do not draw it out from God, but receive it as pure gratuitous love.

As with any gift, we must do something with it. The Greek verb for "work out" (κατεργαζομαι) means to "accomplish for yourself" or "bring about to

---

2 Isa. 61:3

3 Seed metaphor is from Marilyn Vancil in *Self to Lose Self to Find: Using the Enneagram to Uncover Your True, God-gifted Self.*

4 Col. 3:10

5 1 Cor. 15:42

completion."[6] For example, my youngest son Ezekiel just received a Super Heroes Lego set for his birthday. It was a free gift from his aunt and uncle that he did not earn, but it did not come assembled. Zeke had to "work out" the instructions and build the set himself. It took a lot of time and effort, but he eventually finished his very own Super Hero Lego set.

The Good News for Peacemakers is that we already have everything we need to become like Christ. For example, the apostle Paul tells the believers at Philippi that a "humble mindset" was *already* theirs in Christ. The right seeds are already present, they simply have to learn the practical methods of tending the gift in their unique soil. Paul encourages believers to meditate on the Christ, who "did not count equality with God a thing to be grasped, but emptied himself, by taking the form of a servant,"[7] and then to work out that same mindset in their relationships with one another. We can ask: Because Jesus served me, how can I serve others? Instead of pointing people to my status, how can I follow Christ's path of downward mobility?

You'll never become what you aren't already becoming. If you want to become an oak of righteousness, it's not going to just happen on its own. You can't become *something* by doing *nothing*. Therefore, decide how you want to become more like Jesus and start becoming that person right now. Work it out!

→ Pray

Father, thank You for loving me too much to let me stay where I am. Forgive me for not having a bigger view of my potential to become like Christ. By grace, You have saved me from myself and given me a new heart with new desires. Help me work out my salvation with fear and trembling.

---

6 "Strong's #2716 - Κατεργάζομαι - Old & New Testament Greek Lexicon," StudyLight.org, accessed November 16, 2020, https://www.studylight.org/lexicons/greek/2716.html.

7 Phil. 2:6-7

Day 25 Reflections:

Why do you sometimes put a lid on your potential?

_____

_____

_____

_____

How would you describe the difference between working for your salvation and working out your salvation?

_____

_____

_____

_____

What kind of person do you want to become? What might need to change in your life for you to become that person?

_____

_____

_____

_____

→ Respond

Do something creative, like cooking or gardening—something where you work out a plan to turn raw materials into a finished product. Journal about what you learn during the process.

Day 26:

Sailing With the Spirit

The wind blows where it wishes, and you hear its sound, but you do not

know where it comes from or where it goes. So it is with everyone who is born

of the Spirit.

—John 3:8

THE RANKS OF FAITH TRADITIONS THE WORLD over are full of Peacemakers. They are naturally drawn to religious circles that allow them to serve and be part of something bigger than themselves. Unafraid of paradox and mystery due to their penchant for seeing all sides,[1] Peacemakers are generous and humble participants of many worshiping communities. You might find them pushing for ecumenical unity between Christian denominations or seeking common ground among other religious traditions. You might find them enjoying long conversations about theology, philosophy, or their intersection with science. Peacemakers love living in the realm of ideas.

> We cannot direct the wind, but we can adjust the sails.
>
> –Author Unknown

---

1 Cron and Stabile, *The Road*, 87.

Nines love contemplating divine things rather than taking action.[2] The church's history is full of those who pursued the *via contemplativa* over the *via activa*, but the greatest example—Jesus through our most storied saints—found a balance between the two. Our spiritual growth must include thinking and *doing*.

The process of sanctification (becoming more like Christ) is a lot like sailing. In a sailboat, the wind is the driving force. Actually, the Greek word for "wind," *pneuma*, is the same used for *spirit*. The apostle Paul says things like we "are being transformed. ... for this comes from the Lord, who is the Spirit,"[3] or we "walk by the Spirit,"[4] or are "led by the Spirit."[5] Here's the big idea: While the self-awareness offered by tools like the Enneagram can outline our path toward becoming, they are not sufficient to enact the change within. We need an external, transcendent power source.

Sailing is not a passive activity; you must do the work of setting the sails and holding the ropes as the wind blows into them. Similarly, the receptor of God's power must be prepared. In essence, sailing is an activity that requires participation from both the sailor and the wind. Together, making use of your tools and the freely-given wind, you can go distances that wouldn't have been possible under your own strength.

> You must do the work of setting the sails and holding the ropes as the Spirit blows into them.

The Enneagram teaches that when a Peacemaker is secure and healthy, you will inhabit the Achiever's best qualities. Using the strengths of planning and goal-setting to properly set your heart's sails, you will catch the power you need to integrate the spiritual disciplines into your life. Examples include meditation, prayer, solitude, fasting, study, service, confession, and celebration.

Pastor John Fooshee offers the following practical recommendations:

---

2 Wagner, *Nine Lenses.*

3 2 Cor. 3:18

4 Gal. 5:16

5 Gal. 5:18

- Spend more time in nature, communing with God while hiking, camping, gardening, or walking. "When life becomes overwhelming with conflict, the outdoors offer rest and the assurance that God is the source of balance and order."[6]

- Set a fixed hour of prayer and stick to it. "Stopping at regular times throughout the day encourages consistency … and requires your full participation, helping you enter into the peaceful presence of Jesus."

- Start the practice of journaling so you can become more aware of your desires, anger, blessings, burdens, and calling—and be able to share them more easily with others.

- Start a Bible reading plan to push yourself to remain consistently anchored in God's Word.

Find a place to serve so that you can take pleasure in being connected to the whole and build others up.[7]

The Good News for Peacemakers is that the Holy Spirit is always moving. Take comfort that you can use your gifts to do the work, learn the disciplines, and wield the tools. However, we all must ultimately wait to be carried along by the winds of the Holy Spirit. It won't always be smooth sailing, but God will pilot your journey.

→ Pray

Father, it is You who works in me, both to will and to work for Your good pleasure. You oversee my spiritual formation and will bring it to completion. Help me to do what only I can do (set the sails) so that You can do what only You can do (change my heart and take me home).

---

6   Riso and Hudson, *Personality Types*, 350.

7   People Launching, "Gospel Enneagram," Gospel Enneagram, 2020, https://www.gospelenneagram.com.

Day 26 Reflections:

Describe a time when you "caught wind" of the Spirit and were consistent in one or more spiritual disciplines. What happened? How did you feel?

What about yielding control of your life to the Spirit terrifies you? Relieves you?

What can you do to build the spiritual disciplines above into your current weekly rhythms?

→ Respond

Find a book on spiritual disciplines and add it to your reading list.

Day 27:

The Stubborn Prophet

Now the word of the Lord came to Jonah the son of Amittai, saying, "Arise, go to

Nineveh, that great city, and call out against it, for their evil has come up before

me." But Jonah rose to flee to Tarshish from the presence of the Lord.

—Jonah 1:1-3

WHEN YOU ARE PRESSURED TO DO SOMETHING and you don't want to do it, do you dig your heels in or run in the opposite direction? The prophet Jonah (who could easily be known as "the stubborn prophet") knows just how you feel.

Jonah receives marching orders from God to go to Nineveh with a warning message about the impending destruction for their wickedness. He doesn't like this unpleasant assignment and immediately jumps on a ship to Tarshish—the furthest destination in the opposite direction. However, God soon begins to rock his boat by bringing a storm so strong it causes the seasoned sailors to panic and fear for their lives. Jonah finally comes out of hiding and, after the lot of honesty, admits his

> Stubbornness is the strength of the weak.
>
> –Johann Kaspar Lavater[1]

---

1   Carrie Mason-draffen, *151 Quick Ideas to Deal With Difficult People: Easyread Edition* (N.p.: Booksurge Llc, 2008), 113.

stubbornness against the Creator God is causing this upheaval. In the end, Jonah suggests the sailors toss him overboard to save their lives.

In a surprising twist, Jonah does not drown, but is swallowed by a giant fish. Now, this may sound horrendous, but it is actually an act of God's mercy. The fish has God-given orders to ship Jonah first-class to the nearest shore. Once Jonah arrives in dramatic fashion, the Ninevites hear about God's coming destruction and—to our great surprise and his—the city repents. Jonah, upset at the prospect of his nation's greatest enemies receiving forgiveness, tells God he wants to die.

Why is Jonah not excited about making the top 10 most successful prophets list? Because he knows exactly what will happen to his enemies: "That is why I made haste to flee to Tarshish; for I knew that you are a gracious God and merciful, slow to anger and abounding in steadfast love, and relenting from disaster."[2] Jonah wasn't excited about going back to his homeland to tell them their enemies were still alive because of him.[3]

> When Peacemakers feel coerced, they dig in their heels and take control of the situation through *nonaction.*

The story of this reluctant prophet illustrates some of the themes that are prevalent in an unhealthy Peacemaker. We see a spiritual slothfulness or even defiance in embracing God's divine assignment. Like an ostrich sticking its head in the sand or an angry toddler, Jonah closes his heart and ears and pretends not to hear God's voice. This apathy toward the Ninevites extends even to his own life at the end of the story, by being unwilling to believe in the worth of those he was raised to fear.

When Peacemakers feel coerced, they dig in their heels and take control of the situation through *nonaction.*[4] Beatrice Chestnut explains, "Like Eights, Nines don't like to be told what to do, but they are quieter about it, and if they feel overly

---

2   Jon. 4:2

3   Richard Rohr and Andreas Ebert, *The Enneagram: A Christian Perspective*, Kindle edition (Crossroad, 2001), 190-191.

4   Palmer, *The Enneagram in Love and Work*, 238.

controlled or disrespected by someone, they can covertly stop cooperating as a way of asserting themselves without creating open conflict."[5]

An elephant, though it has a gentle disposition, can be impossible to move.[6] Likewise, Peacemakers who are firmly planted in their ways may tune others out and exert massive resistance when asked to do something they don't want to do. As Enneagram coach Callie Ammons says, "Nines are the kings and queens of excuses."[7]

The theme of stubbornness can be traced throughout the Scriptures from Adam and Eve in the Garden, Pharaoh in Egypt, the Israelites at Mt. Sinai, and the tradition-bound Pharisees in Jesus' day. Stubbornness both surrounds and still lurks within us. Our spiritual stubbornness leads us to put up walls to keep ourselves safe. In doing so, we shut out God and others. So, the apostle Paul issues a warning in his letter to the Romans that we will all be held accountable for our stubbornness before a righteous Judge.[8]

The Good News for Peacemakers is that God is stubbornly merciful. His grace is sufficient to cover evil Nineveh, as well as a prophet's rebellious heart. Because of the covenant He's made with us through the work of Christ, His mercies are renewed every morning for those of us who know what we should do (like Jonah) but don't do it. In radical love and vulnerability, Christ opened His arms to us on the cross so that we could also live with such openness. If we let go of our stubbornness, fear, and pride, and accept God's marching orders today, then our modern-day Ninevahs will be reconciled to a loving God. That kind of faith can move mountains—even if God has to push you overboard once in a while.

---

5   Chestnut, *The 9 Types of Leadership*, 290.

6   Rohr and Ebert, *The Enneagram*, 189.

7   Find Callie Ammons at https://callieammons.com/.

8   Rom. 2:5

→ **Pray**

Father, I praise You for being abundantly merciful to religious Jonahs like me. Thank You for replacing my heart of stone with a heart of flesh.[9] Free me from my stubbornness and hardness of heart. Help me to trust You and submit to Your perfect plan. I know the safest place to be is in the center of Your will.

Day 27 Reflections:

How have you seen yourself be "stubbornly good" toward someone who didn't deserve it?

In what ways do you find yourself relating to Jonah?

What causes you to choose stubbornness? What pain are you trying to prevent?

→ **Respond**

Jot down a request that someone has repeatedly made of you. Now, list one reason why that request may ultimately be from God and what positive results may come about.

9 Ezek. 36:26

Day 28:

Covert Rage

In this is love, not that we have loved God but that he loved us and sent his Son

to be the propitiation for our sins.

—1 John 4:10

IN COLLEGE, MY FRATERNITY PLEDGE CLASS MADE a trip up to Minneapolis to visit the *Sigma Phi Epsilon* chapter there and enjoy the city. Not wanting to pay for a hotel our last night there, we decided to drive the five-plus hours through the night back to Omaha. On the way back, during my turn at the wheel, I kept asking for someone to take over as I grew more tired. I white-knuckled it for a while, but eventually nodded off. Thankfully, the rumble strips woke me up and saved us. I never made that mistake again.

> There is one sort of person who seems to be silent, but inwardly criticizes other people. Such a person is really talking all the time.
>
> —Abba Poeman[1]

Similarly, Peacemakers endanger themselves and their relationships when they fall asleep at the wheel of their anger. Underneath the surface, often subconsciously, the indolence

---

1   Abba Poeman, cited in Yushi Nomura, *Desert Wisdom: The Sayings of the Desert Fathers* (Maryknoll, NY: Orbis, 2001), 83.

of a Peacemaker acts like a circuit breaker. When you become irritated or anxious, sad or resentful, the desire to keep things calm "trips your breaker," keeping you from exploring what's under the hood.[2] This causes unresolved anger to build under the surface. This "ignore and repress" strategy is ultimately unsustainable and your worst fear will eventually come to pass—the volcano within will explode. It's rare, but it happens. As Ian Cron says, "Despite their reputation for being sweet and accommodating, Nines aren't always sticking daisies into rifle barrels."[3]

Professor and therapist Chuck DeGroat teaches in his book *When Narcissism Comes to Church* that unhealthy Peacemakers are prone to a more *covert* narcissism that does not manifest itself loudly or arrogantly, but rather through a "quiet rage." This aspect of narcissism seeps through as quiet judgmentalism or cold-heartedness that

> Peacemakers endanger themselves and their relationships when they fall asleep at the wheel to their anger.

outwardly says "I'm fine," but inwardly seethes, "I want to make you pay." DeGroat pulls on this thread further, explaining where this path may take a Peacemaker if left unchecked:

> "This subtle manipulative power is far more potent than it appears. In the church context, this type of narcissism can stifle communication, connection, and creativity as staff or worship teams or other groups feel the anger that is not being communicated overtly. Without words, this person has the power to force others to quit, resign, or comply. However, because her typical demeanor is pleasant, she can play the victim, pointing the finger at others with the firm belief that she'd never quite have the power to inflict the damage they contend she has inflicted."[4]

How do we protect ourselves from going down this road? Keeping an "anger journal" will help. Additionally, talk to someone regularly whom you can trust. If you are having trouble identifying or sharing these feelings, don't assume they

---

2 Wagner, *Nine Lenses.*

3 Cron and Stabile, *The Road Back to You*, 77.

4 Chuck DeGroat, *When Narcissism Comes to Church: Healing Your Community From Emotional and Spiritual Abuse* (United Kingdom: InterVarsity Press, 2020), 61-62.

aren't there. Ask those whom you love and trust whether they have seen the volcano in action (before and after eruption), find a qualified counselor who can help sort through these internal movements, or try downloading a *Feelings Wheel* to help you identify your emotions.

The Good News for Peacemakers is that we have been "saved by [Jesus] from the wrath of God."[5] Although God disciplines those who belong to Him out of love, He will no longer punish us in anger.[6] Therefore, we don't have any right to punish others; we must let go of the stubbornness of our flesh that wants to mistreat people for walking all over us, a desire which is unquenchable and impossible to satisfy. The alternative is to "let the peace of Christ rule in your hearts."[7]

Share your anger with others as you feel it building. Don't assume they'll reject you, and don't assume you will come off too strong. You have one of the kindest dispositions on the entire spectrum of personalities! Remember, letting off steam does a lot less damage than lava. Even then, if you've erupted on more than one occasion, there is forgiveness and hope.

→ Pray

Father, You are a benevolent and gracious King. Thank You for not giving me what I deserve. Let Your peace rule in my heart and mercy abound on my lips. Heal my hurts so that I don't hurt others. Help me to be "slow to anger and abounding in steadfast love."[8]

---

5 Rom. 5:9

6 Heb. 12:4-11

7 Col. 3:15

8 Ps. 86:15

Day 28 Reflections:

When was the last time you blew up at someone? What long list of felt wrongs, anxieties, and fears led to the eruption?

What resentments are you still carrying? (For example, "I will never forget what they did.")

If propitiation declares that Jesus removed the wrath we all deserve, then how should that change your attitude toward your enemies?

→ Respond

Download a "Feelings Wheel" and identify what primary emotion you've been feeling lately and why.

Day 29:

Bring the Heat

While people are saying, "There is peace and security," then sudden destruction

will come upon them as labor pains come upon a pregnant woman, and they

will not escape. But you are not in darkness, brothers, for that day to surprise

you like a thief. For you are all children of light, children of the day. We are not

of the night or of the darkness. So then let us not sleep, as others do, but let us

keep awake and be sober.

—1 Thessalonians 5:3-6

ARE YOU A THERMOMETER OR A THERMOSTAT? There is a world of difference between the two because, while a thermometer *reads* the temperature in the room, only a thermostat can *regulate* it. A naturally accommodating personality will often lead to reflective fluctuation, like a thermometer. So, Peacemakers must work to be clear on the vision and culture they want, use precise language, over-communicate each day, and use their skill for negotiation to cool down the room when conflict arises or hot-headed personalities make people sweat!

> It is nothing to die; it is frightful not to live.
>
> –Victor Hugo[1]

---

1   Riso and Hudson, *The Wisdom*, 32.

When we planted a church in 2015, our old building had a dying heating and cooling system. When the boilers didn't work, our members had to bring blankets with them to Sunday worship. Oh, the joy of church planting! Occasionally, the heat would kick on and you could feel the atmosphere change—people would stand up, sing louder, and raise their hands as the heat filled the room. Likewise, when Peacemakers "bring the heat," they can instill warmth and productivity into a cold or lethargic environment.

The apostle Paul tells the Thessalonian church that paying attention to their future will determine how they live in the present. Though the "Day of the Lord" will come imminently, some people are still living as though drunk, operating with a false sense of peace and security, and stumbling blindly, aimless and without concern for the future. Paul urges them, "So then let us not sleep, as others do, but let us keep awake and be sober."[2]

> You were not created to be a *wallflower* but a witness in the world.

The lie you're led to believe is this: "I won't be safe if I'm assertive or accessible." If you buy into this lie, you'll settle for the imaginary world of "false peace and security," adopting a "play dead to stay alive" strategy. Therefore, the path of growth is pursuing the virtue of *engagement*:[3] you were not created to be a *wallflower* but a *witness* in the world.

Engagement first requires us to reject "an attitude of taking oneself lightly in order not to weigh upon others."[4] Naranjo teaches that Nines may try and take the "heat off" conversations "by being abstract rather than specific, by not getting the point, by coming up with bad examples or none at all, by politeness instead of directness, by stereotyped language instead of original language, by substituting mild emotions for intense ones, by talking about rather than talking to, and by shrugging off the importance of what one just said."[5]

---

2   1 Thess. 5:6

3   McCord, *The Enneagram Type 9*, 133.

4   Claudio Naranjo, *Character and Neurosis: An Integrative View* (United States: Gateways/IDHHB, 1994), 234.

5   Ibid, 236.

Engagement requires us to not hit the "snooze button" throughout the day, where mental withdrawal keeps our hearts and minds asleep at home while our bodies remain in the room. Or we may withdraw in more obvious ways: becoming magician-like, performing "disappearing acts," leaving others asking, "Where did they go?"

Drew Moser points out that having a "past" orientation to time plays a factor in a Peacemakers's ability to engage in the present. Musing on past memories provides a calm retreat for the soul, allowing them to leapfrog over present sufferings to future possibilities where there are no conflicts and calmer waters.[6]

The Good News for Peacemakers is that Jesus remains assertive and accessible for our sakes. In Matthew 9, Jesus encounters multiple distractions all in one day (e.g. Jairus, sick woman, two blind men, demon-oppressed man, etc.). Fully present in all these instances, He looks people in the eye, listens to their hearts, walks with them, and offers His wisdom and healing.

Rather than being "everywhere and nowhere," plant yourself *somewhere*. The Holy Spirit will give you all the power you need to set the temperature in every room you walk into. Seek to "work your way" into the center of every group conversation rather than remaining on the fringe. Accept more invitations from people not as interruptions but as divine appointments. Share what you really think without backing down. Don't let others mess with the thermostat when it is your task to set it!

→ Pray

Father, I praise You that I don't have to hide and am fully safe in Your presence. Help me to clear away the distractions and be more assertive and accessible. Thank You for sending Jesus to be the perfect example of being fully present. Because there is joy in Your presence, fill me with Your Spirit to minister to others today out of a heart that's overflowing.

---

6   Moser, *The Enneagram of Discernment*, 145.

Day 29 Reflections:

When do you hit the mental snooze button? What people or circumstances trigger you?

What does the "mental escape" to the past or future look like for you? How does it make you feel?

How would the practice of being fully present satisfy your desire to belong?

→ Respond

Singer-songwriter Ryan O'Neal, known as Sleeping at Last, wrote a song called "Nine" specifically for Peacemakers. Search for and follow along with the lyrics as you listen.

Day 30:

The God Who Declares

For I am God, and there is no other; I am God, and there is none like me,

declaring the end from the beginning and from ancient times things not yet

done, saying, 'My counsel shall stand, and I will accomplish all my purpose,'

calling a bird of prey from the east, the man of my counsel from a far country. I

have spoken, and I will bring it to pass; I have purposed, and I will do it.

—Isaiah 46:9-11

DRIVING IN THE FOG IS NO FUN. In seconds, what was once a clear path has turned into a confusing and disorienting journey, causing us to slow down and desperately search for the lanes, signs, and especially, other vehicles in order to pass through in safety.

> Take care to get what you like, or you will be forced to like what you get.
>
> —George Bernard Shaw[1]

Enneagram coach Beth McCord, a Peacemaker herself, teaches that *this* is what it often feels like in the mind of a Nine: When asked what they want, they often shrug and reply, "I don't know."

---

1   Cloud, *9 Things You Simply Must Do*, 9.

Methodical, internal processing is nothing to apologize for—it just requires more time to get better "visibility" as your feelings, preferences, and solutions come into view. The downside to this, as Drew Moser observes, is that the "Nines' methodical approaches to thought are sometimes too slow for a world that worships efficiency and productivity. This is a shame, for when Nines mentally arrive at a conclusion, it's often worthy of others' consideration."[2]

What can be done to make sure you are heard and not left behind? The first step is learning to *declare* what you want (once you have identified it); make clear what is obscure to others and maybe even yourself. This type of work is incredibly challenging to Peacemakers' subconscious because the message they've heard since childhood is: "It's not okay to assert yourself."[3] It only takes a few unsafe people or memories to put up walls of protection.

If this silent pattern persists and our motto becomes "Let the unspoken remain unsaid,"[4] our internal health and outer relationships will suffer. Peacemakers can be frustrating to work with when they say "yes," but really mean "no"—or when they passively resist others'

> The more you pay attention to yourself, the more others will pay attention to you.

plans without voicing clear objections.[5] It can be tiring for family members or co-workers to constantly do the work of drawing them out when they don't speak up. More assertive personality types become infuriated when they feel manipulated by the Peacemaker into forcing the hard conversations and always ending up as the bad guy.

On the positive side, the work of declaring will help Peacemakers grow more solid in their desires, convictions, and agendas as they reflect the *imago Dei* within. Christian Enneagram teachers Jim Cofield and Richard Plass note that Peacemakers are made in the image of the "God who declares."[6] Throughout the Scriptures, God makes His heart known. It is precisely because God has

---

2   Moser, *The Enneagram of Discernment*, 144.

3   McCord, *The Enneagram Type 9*, 96.

4   Palmer, *The Enneagram in Love and Work*, 235-236.

5   Chestnut, *The 9 Types of Leadership*, 307.

6   Find out more about their ministry here: https://crosspointministry.com/.

disclosed Himself so clearly through Christ that we can have intimacy with Him and flourish under His wisdom.

As His image bearer, you must resist the temptation to hide in plain sight. Instead, "declare" your needs, frustrations, values, and long-term dreams. Identify for others what you believe is missing and share anything else that may be going on inside of you. The more you pay attention to yourself, the more others will pay attention to you.[7]

The Good News for Peacemakers is that we worship a God who has not left the whole world guessing. The heavens declare God's glory,[8] the inspired Scriptures declare His will,[9] the Son declares the Father's heart,[10] and the Holy Spirit declares all that is ours in Christ.[11] As image-bearers, we too must pursue courageous transparency over insecure obscurity.

This week, if you want to get practical, try working on using more "I" statements with a firm voice, upright posture, looking directly at the person, believing that your needs are just as important as theirs. Try to not worry about their response. Instead, express yourself, even in the midst of your own fog—and leave the results to God.

→ Pray

Father, Your invisible attributes have been clearly perceived so that all men are without excuse. Thank You for revealing Yourself to me so plainly. Because You have covered me with Your love and safety, I make myself fully known. By Your Spirit, make me humbly assertive in all that I do today.

---

7   Jeff and Beth McCord, *Becoming Us: Using the Enneagram to Create a Thriving Gospel-Centered Marriage* (United States: Morgan James Publishing, 2019), 144.

8   Ps. 19:1

9   2 Tim. 3:16

10   Heb. 1:1-2

11   John 16:14

Day 30 Reflections:

When was the last time you made yourself clear? How did it feel?

Does your speech reflect that you value yourself as much as you value others?

Why is it tempting for you to obscure your true colors?

God does not withhold Himself from you. How does that truth bless you today?

→ Respond

Before you walk into a meeting today, write out your thoughts and feelings. Drew Moser notes that this practice will help Peacemakers avoid getting passed over in fast-paced meetings where they might not have sufficient time to express themselves.[12]

---

12 Moser, *The Enneagram of Discernment*, 148.

Day 31:

Uncomfortable Truths

Do you think that I have come to give peace on earth? No, I tell you, but

rather division.

—Luke 12:51

WHEN I WAS IN MIDDLE SCHOOL, MY parents were invited into a home Bible study and immediately got hooked. Soon after, they began taking our family to a small church in a neighboring town. The residents of our small town, you could say, were less than enthusiastic about my parents' new denomination. My mother was fired from her teaching job because the private school feared she might proselytize her students, and we received a letter in the mail from an anonymous person in the community who let us know we were no longer welcome. Following Jesus' call as we understood it was the best decision we ever made, but it was not without consequences.

> If we don't stand for something, we'll fall for anything.
> −Irene Dunne[1]

1   Reader's Digest, Volume 47, (July, 1945), 48.

Though we would not wish such experiences on anyone, we also believe that true, lasting peace between ever-warring humanity will not fully and finally prevail until Jesus returns. He said things will get worse before they get better, so we must reset our expectations. If the uncomfortable truths Jesus taught gained Him some enemies, we will have some too. It sounds strange to hear Jesus telling His disciples that He came to bring division rather than peace. Did Jesus' message change? How does His promise of division square with the command "live peaceably with all?"[2]

The life Jesus offers is one of peace. It draws a stark distinction between itself and other paths, and offers little room for argument. On one side is the belief that Jesus "is the way, the truth, and the life."[3] On the other side is the belief that the path to God is through our own achievements and "goodness." An uncomfortable truth such as this one can divide a family.[4]

> Jesus came to redraw the lines of our ultimate authority and allegiance.

How comfortable are you with sharing truths that you know may cause offense? It's not easy for anyone—myself included—but it's especially difficult for Peacemakers who are wired to erase lines in the sand rather than draw them. In fact, Riso and Hudson point out that some Peacemakers tend to gravitate to churches or philosophies which comfort rather than challenge. In addition, they may also edit the teachings of their faith tradition and reframe them in a way that is more palatable to their audience. It is important to note that those who profess both "conservative" and "liberal" views "edit" their faith."[5]

Embracing uncomfortable truths will never feel natural for the Peacemaker, but as long as the kingdom is still pushing back darkness, worldviews will collide. Jesus came to redraw the lines of our ultimate authority and allegiance. Therefore, we submit to God faithfully, knowing peace has no fellowship with darkness.

---

2   Rom. 12:18

3   John 14:6

4   Matt. 10:35

5   Riso and Hudson, *Personality Types*, 342.

The Good News for Peacemakers is that challenging and respecting others can coexist. My friend and fellow pastor, Gavin Johnson, encourages us to *pray* for doors, *check* doors, and *respect* doors. When we pray for doors, we make a list of people that we want to know God as we do. Next, we check doors, throwing out "feelers" by telling others of our life-giving spiritual community and practices or about how our faith informs what we do. Then, we wait to see how they respond. We cultivate a soft heart for the world by asking questions and being good listeners. Lastly, we respect doors. If a door is open, we take advantage of the opportunity and share the hope that we have.[6] If it is apparent that they aren't willing to listen, then we don't need to bust down the door.

God created the world and Christ saturates all things—including those fellow image-bearers we are trying to reach. The Holy Spirit is the One who convicts people, not us! As the founder of Cru, Bill Bright said, "Success in witnessing is simply taking the initiative to share Christ in the power of the Holy Spirit and leaving the results to God."[7]

If you need courage to share life-giving (often uncomfortable) truths today, then just ask! The apostle Paul asked the Ephesian church to pray for him so that he would declare the truth with boldness "as I ought to speak."[8] If Paul needed prayer for boldness, how much more do we?

→ Pray

Father, my ultimate allegiance is with You. Help me to embrace and proclaim Your uncomfortable truths as part of my peace-making strategy. Give me the boldness to draw lines wherever they are needed and to accept the fact that there will be divisions as You unite all things under Your Son, the Prince of Peace.

---

6   1 Pet. 3:15

7   Crutweets, "How You Can Be A Fruitful Witness: Cru," Cru.org, accessed November 16, 2020, https://www.cru.org/us/en/train-and-grow/transferable-concepts/be-a-fruitful-witness.6.html.

8   Eph. 6:20

Day 31 Reflections:

How does an absence of truth lead to an absence of peace? How did Jesus' confrontations make way for peace?

What feels difficult or uncomfortable about confronting others?

Who would you like to share the truth with? What is stopping you?

→ Respond

"Check the door" with someone today by asking a question such as: "Were you raised in a religious home? Have you had any negative experiences with organized religion? Are you experiencing any difficulty right now in your life? How can I pray for you?"

Day 32:

Stress Triggers

And Moses lifted up his hand and struck the rock with his staff twice, and water

came out abundantly, and the congregation drank, and their livestock. And the

Lord said to Moses and Aaron, "Because you did not believe in me, to uphold

me as holy in the eyes of the people of Israel, therefore you shall not bring this

assembly into the land that I have given them."

—Numbers 20:11-12

WHAT ARE YOUR MOST COMMON STRESS TRIGGERS? Have you ever reached a breaking point that led to a total shutdown? While this eventually happens to all people, the good news Riso and Hudson share about Peacemakers is that they have a higher tolerance than most for stress and irritation. They tend not to fly off the handle over the little things, but remain (at least outwardly) relaxed, patient, and understanding.[2]

> No pressure, no diamonds.
>
> –Thomas Carlyle[1]

---

1   Iam A. Freeman, *Seeds of Revolution: A Collection of Axioms, Passages and Proverbs, Volume 1* (United Kingdom: iUniverse, 2014), 74.

2   Riso and Hudson, *Personality Types,* 349.

Peacemakers are human just like the rest of us. Beatrice Chestnut shares some of the most common triggers in her book, *The 9 Types of Leadership*.[3] She says that from being unexpectedly put in the spotlight or singled out, to feeling pressure to do something without clearly stated expectations, or being rushed to make a decision (especially when critical feedback is likely to result), your type is most negatively activated. In doing these things, Peacemakers are not allowed time and space to think or aren't given a clear opportunity to say no. This necessity for "mental elbow room" becomes clearer when you find yourself having a difficult time getting into a group conversation while everyone is talking or giving strong opinions.

This frustration of feeling left out or overlooked can grow when members of the group strike out on their own or overlook your possible contributions, taking your reticence for a lack of opinion or relevant skill and experience. When you are triggered, you may try to convince yourself that you are okay or give others the impression that you are okay. This can lead to a total shutdown or worse—a public meltdown. A stressed Peacemaker may become reactive, insecure, blaming, defensive, paranoid, and be subject to temper tantrums or outbursts.[4]

> Jesus was struck at the cross but reverberated compassion.

Under severe pressure, Nines may oppose people openly or slip into "analysis paralysis" as they think of all the worst-case scenarios or consequences. Blame can easily be turned from themselves to others if they feel like they were taken advantage of or victimized by aggressive people or bad authority.[5]

The Bible presents many case studies of people who, because of stress, shut down completely or had a public meltdown. One of those whose failure was *very* visible (and came with steep consequences) is Moses. More than once, he seems to throw up his hands, telling God he would rather die than deal with the Israelites another

---

3   Chestnut, *The 9 Types of Leadership*, 295-297.

4   Riso and Hudson, *Personality Types*, 366.

5   Palmer, *The Enneagram in Love and Work*, 234-235.

moment. While the shutdowns often occur in private, Moses' public meltdowns occur in front of the entire nation, as at Meribah, when he strikes the rock.[6]

Moses had a very stressful job—in the hot desert for over 40 years, no less! It's certainly understandable that he sometimes bends past the breaking point. He listens to constant complaining, bickering, and backsliding. Moses' leadership and authority are under constant threat by his own friends and family. We hear often of his self-doubt, frustration, loneliness, and anger. His final public failure at Meribah is the stated reason he is denied entry to the promised land. Nonetheless, Moses always recovers and stands with his people, leading them to the doorstep of Canaan.

The Good News for Peacemakers is that there is a way to bend without breaking. With proper care for your mental health and trusted relationships with those you have given permission to call you out *before* you break down, you can both preserve your reputation and "uphold [God] as holy in the eyes of the people."[7]

Let your stress lead to sanctification—a cleansing. Much as Jesus was struck at the cross but reverberated compassion, your suffering and stress can be the thing that leads you to experience grace in the midst of paralysis or passive-aggressiveness. It can lead to greater empathy and compassion toward the intrusive people around you or dismissive authority over you. Ultimately, stress and sanctification can lead to your being able to see the Divine within everyone you meet.

→ Pray

Father, thank You for sending Your Son to be our example of someone who bent without breaking. Through temptation, opposition, persecution, and even death, He did not fold. Oh Lord, let the same compassion flow out of me that flowed out of Jesus when He was struck on the cross. With Your steadfast patience, I will point my friends and enemies to the promised land of a life lived with You today.

---

6   Num. 20:10-13

7   Num. 20:12

Day 32 Reflections:

How has your high tolerance for stress been an asset at home or in the workplace?

What triggers your stress most often?

Who are the people in your life monitoring your "meltdown meter?"

What steps can you take now to prevent a public meltdown like the one Moses experienced?

→ Respond

Because others may be able to see the warning signs before you do, ask someone to share how they can tell when you are stressed out.

Day 33:

Love Has a Backbone

Let love be genuine. Abhor what is evil; hold fast to what is good.

—Romans 12:9

HATE IS SUCH A STRONG WORD, ISN'T it? You might even have a visceral reaction when you hear the word, but there is such a thing as righteous hate. The wisdom of Proverbs rather bluntly says, "There are six things that the Lord hates ... ."[2] The apostle Paul tells the church in Rome to "abhor what is evil"[3] which literally means to "regard with disgust and hatred."

> Certain things, if not seen as lovely or detestable, are not being correctly seen at all.
>
> – C. S. Lewis[1]

Henry Cloud teaches that righteous hatred helps "us move against certain traits and issues, thus becoming different from them. Think of it as being like the energy that pushes a boat away from a dock. We use the energy of hate to move against that trait so that we are not docked to it. We push away from attaching

1 C. S. Lewis, *A Preface to Paradise Lost* (India: Atlantic Publishers & Distributors (P) Limited, 2005), 50-51.

2 Prov. 6:16

3 Rom. 12:9

ourselves to that thing we hate. This action gives us a real separateness from that trait, so that we do not drag it with us across the sea."[4]

Our physical bodies illustrate this process well. Your immune system is always identifying harmful bacteria or viruses and then moving to attack them in order to keep your other cells protected.[5] Similarly, you must name unhealthy spiritual traits within so you can push away from them. If your soul remains indifferent to these threats, your overall spiritual health will be in jeopardy.

Sometimes, these threats are external—the result of an unhealthy trait in someone you are in relationship with. When this is the case, you must—however uncomfortable you may feel— verbally request that they take action, for their sake as much as yours. For example, in the Bible, we read about a prophet named Hosea who God told to marry a prostitute named Gomer—a woman who sold herself over and over again for money. The purpose of this marriage was to illustrate the relational dynamic of the Israelites' marriage to God—namely, His faithfulness and their lack thereof. As you might expect, Hosea's marriage to Gomer didn't start off very well. Gomer cheated on Hosea and was unfaithful to him, running back to the life she knew. No matter how unhealthy our negative traits and relationships are, we also frequently go back to the comfortability of the known.

> Love will not tolerate evil when it is supported by the backbone of truth.

Hosea wasn't going to tolerate it. Right after he paid all that he had to redeem his wife, he says, "You must dwell as mine for many days. You shall not play the whore, or belong to another man."[6] In this interaction, Hosea illustrates an important aspect of God-like love: "Love has a backbone."[7] Put simply, real love will not tolerate evil when it is supported by the backbone of truth.

This doesn't mean you have to be harsh with others and give up that trademark kindness others have come to love. Having a backbone does not mean overreacting

---

4   Cloud, *9 Things You Simply Must Do*, 144.

5   Ibid, 145.

6   Hosea 3:3

7   Bryan Loritts, *Insider Outsider: My Journey as a Stranger in White Evangelicalism and My Hope for Us All* (United States: Zondervan, 2018), 171.

or suddenly blasting people with truth. Rather, it looks like "going hard on the issue, and soft on the person."[8] Much like our immune system—which sends out antibodies to fight the infection without attacking the rest of the body—we must identify the *true* threat to personal and relational well-being. In the same way, Peacemakers can raise awareness about an "infection" caused by sin without destroying the person or the relationship in the process."[9]

The Good News for Peacemakers is that God is the Master Surgeon who carefully and precisely removes our unhealthy attitudes and behaviors without causing harm to us! As recipients of divine healing, we've been released to protect the body of Christ by speaking truth to the power of evil.

Remember, your spiritual health is dependent upon what you love and hate. Just as our physical bodies would not survive long if they were not vigilant, tell your soul today to care deeply about the things God has declared unhealthy for you.

→ Pray

Father, the story of Hosea and Gomer proves how faithful You've been to us even when we are faithless. Thank You for sending Jesus to be my brother and example in showing love for the world without allowing evil to grow in His or others' hearts. Help me to show others the same tough love and mercy You've given me so that Your church can flourish.

---

8   Cloud, *9 Things You Simply Must Do*, 153.

9   Ibid, 160-161.

Day 33 Reflections:

What kinds of evil do you hate?

What have you tolerated for far too long (in yourself or someone else)?

What do you think it means to “go hard” on an issue but “soft on the person”?

→ Respond

Unhealthy people need a written diagnosis to get healthy. Give yourself a spiritual diagnosis by writing down specific attitudes, habits, or behaviors that are causing irritation or frustration.

Day 34:

Necessary Endings

I am the true vine, and my Father is the vinedresser. Every branch in me that does not bear fruit he takes away, and every branch that does bear fruit he prunes, that it may bear more fruit.

—John 15:1-2

DO YOU TEND TO PROCRASTINATE FIXING THINGS that are broken? I once waited an entire year to get my fractured tooth pulled, and let me tell you, I suffered through many meals that year! Even now, the check engine light is on in my van, but I've been waiting to take it in because I'm afraid of the scope of the problem. Can you relate?

> Every new beginning comes from some other beginning's end.
>
> –Seneca, Roman philosopher[1]

Any temporary disruption to our peace will prevent us from just "pulling the tooth," because we will do anything to return to equilibrium as quickly as possible. What eventually pushes us over the edge to finally do something is when "the pain of staying the same becomes greater

---

1 Peter Scazzero, *The Emotionally Healthy Leader: How Transforming Your Inner Life Will Deeply Transform Your Church, Team, and the World* (United States: Zondervan, 2015), 280.

than the pain of changing."[2] Puttering along with the check engine light on is not the life Jesus intended for us. As Henry Cloud explains:

> "[Healthy] people get rid of bad stuff. Period. Sometimes quickly and sometimes through a process, but they get rid of it. They get it out of their hair, off their plate, out of their souls, and out of their lives. They do not allow negative things to take up space in their lives, draining them of energy and resources. If the tooth is infected, they pull it. Immediately. They have little tolerance for nagging pains that are unresolved. They finish off problems and do not allow them to remain."[3]

The biblical language for this process is calling *pruning*. The world is a garden, Jesus is the vine, and the Father is the vinedresser. The Father not only cuts off the *fruitless* branches, but prunes the *fruitful* ones. Pruning is not comfortable but it is a necessary process that involves cutting sick, dead, or overgrown branches. As it is with the physical world, so it is with our souls; we must recognize those aspects of our lives that are not facilitating life, whether they be relationships, activities, beliefs, or possessions.

> There are things that must die so we can truly live.

Solomon said there is "a time to keep and a time to cast away."[4] So why is it so hard for us to let some things go so new branches can grow? Being oriented to the past, Peacemakers can become nostalgic about relationships they've merged with or the traditions they've been raised in. Reflecting on the past can become a sentimental source of happiness and solidity when chaos hits; simply, the past is less threatening than the future.[5] Furthermore, Peacemakers may idealize those they merge with or live with a false sense of hope: "If I wait it out, things will get better, or they will change." However, what you need is *concrete* hope. If the objective data doesn't lead you to conclude that things will change six months or one year from now, it must be pruned—it has to go. These things must have their necessary ending, or you will come to the *end* of yourself.

---

2   Peter Scazzero and Warren Bird. *The Emotionally Healthy Church* (Grand Rapids: Zondervan, 2015), 76.

3   Cloud, *9 Things You Simply Must Do*, 45-46.

4   Eccl. 3:6

5   Riso and Hudson, *Personality Types*, 355.

The Good News for Peacemakers is that God will give you new things if your hands aren't too full to receive them. We often miss the invitation to open the door to new beginnings because we haven't embraced the theological truth of necessary endings. As author Peter Scazzero reminds us, "Death is a necessary prelude to resurrection."[6] It was through Jesus' death that our new life began. Likewise, there are things that must die so we can truly live. It will be hard to let go and you will grieve but joy always comes in the morning.[7]

→ Pray

Father, You are the vinedresser who will complete the good work You started in me. You say that a true disciple will bear fruit. Help me to live more frutifully by taking action to prune my life and relationships. Give me the faith to believe that resurrection life will come out of necessary endings.

---

6 Scazzero, *The Emotionally Healthy Leader*, 274.

7 Ps. 30:5

Day 34 Reflections:

What do you need to release?

_____

_____

_____

_____

Where in your life have you been living with false hope that things will change?

_____

_____

_____

_____

When it comes to your schedule, what are you doing that may be "permissible but not beneficial"?

_____

_____

_____

_____

→ Respond

Write out briefly what you want to be true of your life five years from now versus what it will actually look like if you don't let go of the things you know you need to leave behind.

Day 35:

Proactive Parenting

Hear, O Israel: The Lord our God, the Lord is one. You shall love the Lord your

God with all your heart and with all your soul and with all your might. And

these words that I command you today shall be on your heart. You shall teach

them diligently to your children, and shall talk of them when you sit in your

house, and when you walk by the way, and when you lie down, and when

you rise.

—Deuteronomy 6:4-7

Peacemakers make incredible parents, caregivers, mentors, and considerate leaders. A healthy, mature Nine will be your best supporter and cheerleader. They will listen well, model unconditional love, stand by your side through every season, celebrate your accomplishments, and create a "sanctuary of peace" in your shared space.

> To be in your children's memories tomorrow, you have to be in their lives today.
>
> –Barbara Johnson[1]

Author Jacqui Pollock, who helps people understand their parenting personality

---

1 Barbara Johnson, *The Best Devotions of Barbara Johnson* (United States: Zondervan, 2010), 109.

through the Enneagram, adds that Peacemaking parents naturally make their children feel accepted, help them appreciate other people's points of view, provide a safe and calming presence, and are very reliable. They are also less prone to putting undue pressure on their children as many overly-competitive parents do.[2]

When Peacemakers are unhealthy, however, the three things to watch out for are *passive-aggressiveness, procrastination,* and *permissiveness.* Random bursts of anger, snide remarks, or bouts of the silent treatment may be confusing or frightening for young children. Under heavy stress, Nines may also find themselves on the couch or in bed unable to fulfill their high-priority responsibilities, or their tendency to avoid conflict may lead to procrastination rather than attacking important issues head on. Lastly, Nines may set aside the authoritative role, merge with the children's agenda, and become too permissive in allowing the children to do what they want to do.[3]

> Saying *yes* to God often means saying *no* to our children.

Saying *yes* to God often means saying *no* to our children, and though their young hearts may perceive it as a lack of caring, we know from experience that our loving firmness can offer firm grounding in a world that is perpetually unsettling. It's been said, "God loves us just as we are, but He loves us too much to let us stay that way." Therefore, remember that teaching the children in our lives to love God with their heart and soul, mind, and strength, and to live under His reign and rule is God's definition of success.

As we look to the Bible, we find King David thriving as a spiritual leader but struggling as a father. Amnon, Absalom, Adonijah, and Solomon go on to worship idols, gather a harem of lovers, and do unspeakable things.

Eunice, on the other hand, has a very different legacy as a parent. Eunice is present in her son, Timothy's, life and teaches him about Jesus. She inherits a sincere (non-hypocritical) faith from her mother Lois and faithfully passes it on to her son. From Timothy's childhood on, Eunice diligently teaches him the

---

2 Pollock, Jacqui., Loftus, Margaret., Tresidder, Tracy. *Knowing Me, Knowing Them: Understand Your Parenting Personality by Discovering the Enneagram* (Australia: Monterey Press, 2014), 154-155.

3 Ibid, 155-158.

Bible.[4] Because of her involvement as a parent, young Timothy goes on to leave a spiritual legacy by becoming a traveling ministry partner of the apostle Paul, who entrusts Timothy with important ministry assignments that lay the foundation for the early church.

The Good News for Peacemakers is that, though we are imperfect parents, caregivers, mentors, and leaders, God is our perfect Father whose love never ceases toward us. He is never too busy, tired, or distracted, and never fails to extend the hand of loving acceptance to His children. Just as Jesus received children with open arms, so must we. As you prioritize investing in children, remember these strategies for growth from Jacqui Pollock:

First, provide clearer directives by knowing what you want and sharing it: "What I really think is ... " and "What I'd like you to do is ... ." Second, beware of the things that distract you so that you don't procrastinate the smaller tasks that build up and cause stress. And third, beware of your tendency to merge with your children's lives and live through them. By drawing better boundaries you'll enable your children to live with a greater sense of independence and set them up for success in the world.[5]

→ Pray

Father, help me to cling to the promise that if I train children up in the way they should go, then they will not depart from it when they get old. Fill me with Your Holy Spirit so that the children around me will see the gospel of Your love in action in their own lives. Let my greatest achievement be loving and accepting others just as You have loved me.

---

4   2 Tim. 1:5; 2 Tim. 3:14-15

5   Pollock, *Knowing Me, Knowing Them*, 161-164.

Day 35 Reflections:

How have your unique strengths positively impacted the children in your life?

How have you seen passive-aggressiveness, procrastination, or permissiveness negatively affect the children in your life?

What opportunities are there in your home, extended family, or church community to teach and model the gospel for children or teens?

→ Respond

If you are a parent, schedule a consistent weekly "date" with each of your children, and let them pick the place and activity. If you aren't a parent, look for an opportunity to come alongside a family this week and offer your support!

Day 36:

Love Does

But be doers of the word, and not hearers only, deceiving yourselves. For if anyone is a hearer of the word and not a doer, he is like a man who looks intently at his natural face in a mirror. For he looks at himself and goes away and at once forgets what he was like.

—James 1:22-24

I used to think being loved was the greatest thing to think about, but now I know love is never satisfied just thinking about it.

–Bob Goff[1]

ONE AFTERNOON I ENDED UP ON THE shoulder of the interstate in my wife, Lindsey's, Geo Prizm. Minutes before, the engine began making clanking noises. Soon, the poor car sputtered its last breath as I pulled off the road and remembered the oil change I'd been "meaning" to do for months. The hard part for me was that I told Lindsey that I'd take care of the oil change but didn't. Now, it was too late to act.

Actions speak louder than words. In His parable of the two sons, Jesus forces the religious elite to

---

1   Bob Goff and Donald Miller. *Love Does: Discover a Secretly Incredible Life in an Ordinary World* (United States: Thomas Nelson, 2012), 17.

confront their own inaction on behalf of the people.[2] The father tells his first son to go and work in the vineyard, and though the son gives a hasty no, he thinks better of it and does the work. The second son agreed to do the work but never got around to it. "Which of the two did the will of his father?" Jesus asks His debate partners, and they grudgingly answer: the first.[3]

Love is a verb. Or, as author Bob Goff simply puts it: "*Love does.*" Likewise, the apostle James calls us to be *doers* of the Word, rather than merely *hearers*. The Bible was *not* written to be an intellectual exercise or an FYI; rather, it is a catalogue of and exhortation to radical transformation—an FYT (for your transformation), if you will. This means, as my friend and fellow pastor Gavin Johnson explains, "spiritual maturity is measured by the lag time between knowledge and obedience." The more mature your love for God, the less time it will take to see it come alive in the world and people around you.

> Being a doer of the Word leads to greater satisfaction than our well-intentioned fantasies.

Peacemakers have been known to get stuck in "cruise control," riding the wave of others' conversations, yet remaining quietly uncommitted to following through.[4] Similarly, Riso and Hudson describe this withdrawn stance: "Nines may well have feelings for their loved ones, or even for strangers and animals in distress, but their feelings do not connect with meaningful action. Increasingly, their relationships occur primarily in their imaginations."[5] Furthermore, when Nines *do* get out of their heads, their energy may get diffused toward "a lot of little things," like the dishes, lawn work, house repairs, or errands rather than being focused on personal engagement or other more taxing tasks. You'll need to make sure you don't use busyness as a way to put off doing the things others truly need from you.[6]

---

2 Cf. Matt. 23:3-4

3 Matt. 21:28-32

4 Ibid, 237.

5 Riso and Hudson, *The Wisdom*, 327.

6 Palmer, *The Enneagram in Love and Work*, 235-236.

The Good News for Peacemakers is that God invites you and me into His unfolding plan of redemption as partners, not passive-recipients. As image-bearers, we are called to receive His love and to *imitate* Him in doing it. James reminds us that a "doer who acts, he will be blessed in his doing."[7] Being a doer of the Word leads to greater satisfaction than our well-intentioned fantasies. The reason we have been swept away by our Father's love is that He put Jesus in motion toward us: to heal the hurting, feed the hungry, raise the dead, drive out demons, and physically suffer for us on the cross. Jesus perfectly displayed a *doing* love. Remember that you were saved by Him not to remain lukewarm with good intentions but rather to become a doer of good works.

→ Pray

Father, I know that You love me because of all Your merciful and mighty deeds. Help me to not only love You with my heart and mind, but also with my soul and strength. Fill me with Your Spirit, so that I may fully show up in the world today and actively partner with You in declaring and demonstrating Your love.

---

7   James 1:25

Day 36 Reflections:

How have you noticed the tendency to withdraw to stay unaffected by life?

How do the idealized friendships or relationships in your head differ from actual life?

What can you do to shorten the lag time between knowing and doing?

➜ Respond

Whether you get inspired at home or are listening to a great sermon, get into the habit of writing out your action steps so you don't forget them. You can use a journal or note taking app to keep an ongoing list to review weekly.

Day 37:

Clothed With Power

He gives power to the faint, and to him who has no might he increases strength.

Even youths shall faint and be weary, and young men shall fall exhausted; but

they who wait for the Lord shall renew their strength; they shall mount up with

wings like eagles; they shall run and not be weary; they shall walk and not faint.

—Isaiah 40:29-31

WE LIVE IN A PANDEMIC OF POWER grabs. Worldly power is exerted upon us every day by individuals, corporations, agencies, and yes, religious institutions who seek to use, manipulate, or dominate us for their own ends. As a result of these abuses, it's not surprising that many of us assume all use of power is corrupt.

[Power] is what enables us to make things happen or not.

–Richard Gula[1]

The Bible talks a lot about the topic of power. Consider these passages:

• "For God gave us a spirit not of fear but of power ... ."[2]

1   Richard M. Gula, *Just Ministry: Professional Ethics for Pastoral Ministers* (United States: Paulist Press, 2010), 123.

2   2 Tim. 1:7

- "But you will receive power when the Holy Spirit has come upon you... ."[3]

- "For the kingdom of God does not consist in talk but in power."[4]

- "But stay in the city until you are clothed with power from on high."[5]

Sociologist Dr. James Davison Hunter suggests two reasons that some American Christians have failed to influence our culture: presence and power.

He notes that we've failed to have a faithful presence in the world. Hunter asserts that "the main reason why [some] Christian believers today have not had the influence in the culture to which they have aspired is not that they don't believe enough, or try hard enough, or care enough, or think Christianly enough, or have the right worldview, but rather because they have been absent from the arenas in which the greatest influence in culture is exerted." He also recognizes that some of us have failed to show up in the world making use of our God-given power. Why is this? Wielding power always generates *resistance*—the very thing Peacemakers try to avoid at all costs.

> Jesus displayed a different kind of power that was submissive, humble, and noncoercive.

However, the dynamic of power cannot be avoided. Peter Scazzero, in his book *The Emotionally Healthy Leader*, points out that we have *positional power* (from a title or role we carry), *personal power* (from our gifts, knowledge, and education), *"God-factor" power* (from the sacred authority we've been given by God), *projected power* (from what others unconsciously project onto us), *relational power* (from people entrusting their fears and secrets to us), and *cultural power* (from age, gender, ethnicity, or geography).[6] His big idea is this: whether or not we are technically "in charge" in all of these spaces, we have a lot more power than we think. Why is it absolutely essential for you to think about these categories and take inventory of your power? Scazzero explains:

---

3   Acts 1:8

4   1 Cor. 4:20

5   Luke 24:49

6   Scazzero, *The Emotionally Healthy Leader*, 245-247.

"In my years of teaching and mentoring leaders, I've seen just as much damage result from … leaders who are ambivalent and uncomfortable with their power. Perhaps it's because I identify with them. For these leaders, it somehow feels wrong and unbiblical to grab the reins and take charge because power implies privilege, a higher social status, being above others. The thought of having power as a leader sounds detached and cold. So they prefer to deny or minimize the very real power they have. Some may even feel unworthy or afraid to exercise power, especially in God's name. As a result, they live in a fog, feeling powerless internally, yet responsible to exercise power to lead others."[7]

Rather than ignoring or minimizing your power, you must assert your authority in the power of the Holy Spirit to maximize your influence and minimize chaos. Scazzero points out that when we are reluctant to exercise our power, we open the door for the wrong people to assert themselves and cause harm in our circles of influence.

The Good News for Peacemakers is that we've been given the good gift of power with the ability to steward it in the right time, in the right way, and for the right purposes. Jesus used His divine power to disarm all forms of worldly power through His death and resurrection, triumphing over them in victory.[8] He displayed a different kind of power that was submissive, humble, and noncoercive. Jesus exercised His power under the authority of His Father—setting aside His status and privileges—and selflessly served the good of all.[9] We too have been "clothed with power" to push back darkness. We didn't earn this power but we must steward it.

---

7 Ibid, 243.

8 Col. 2:15

9 John 12:49-50, Phil. 2:6, Luke 17:12-19, John 4:7-26

→ Pray

Father, oh the immeasurable greatness of Your power toward us who believe![10] I praise Jesus for being crucified in weakness so that I would be able to live by the power of God with Him forever.[11] Help me not to be afraid of the power given to me by the Holy Spirit but to make use of it to make things happen today.

Day 37 Reflections:

How have you witnessed cultural or spiritual leaders abusing their power?

What is frightening or challenging about the idea of asserting power?

What has God given you the power and authority to do?

→ Respond

Name your sources of power using Scazzero's help: What formal positions do you hold? What gifts, skills, and assets has God given you? What people or groups have given you permission to speak into their lives? What power do you have based on your age, ethnicity, gender, or other cultural factors?[12]

---

10   Eph. 1:19

11   2 Cor. 13:4

12   Scazzero, *The Emotionally Healthy Leader*, 248-249.

Day 38:

The Discipline of Celebration

Bless the LORD, O my soul, and all that is within me, bless his holy name!

Bless the LORD, O my soul, and forget not all his benefits, who forgives all your

iniquity, who heals all your diseases, who redeems your life from the pit, who

crowns you with steadfast love and mercy, who satisfies you with good so that

your youth is renewed like the eagle's.

—Psalm 103:1-5

WHAT HAS GOD DONE IN YOUR LIFE this week? Gratefulness for what God did yesterday is the fuel you need to keep you positive and energized today. However, this fuel can only be gained through the discipline of celebration—the continual remembrance of what God is doing in you, through you, and around you. Since its earliest days, the church has gathered in remembrance to celebrate with thanksgiving Christ's giving of His body and blood for the life of the world.[2]

> The opposite of home is not distance, but forgetfulness.
>
> –Elie Wiesel[1]

1   Beatrice Chestnut, *The Complete Enneagram: 27 Paths to Greater Self-Knowledge* (Berkeley, CA: She Writes Press, 2013), 57.

2   Acts 2:42

For millennia, we have not ceased to do this supreme act of remembrance through communion—because we forget.

Claudio Naranjo taught that forgetfulness for the Peacemaker is connected to their vice of *indolence*. Indolence is a laziness of the spirit, a loss of an interior self, and a refusal to look closely at oneself or God.[3] That is why the Psalmist exhorts us to "forget not" our God who forgives, heals, redeems, crowns, and satisfies. In the same vein, Moses commanded the people of Israel, "Only take care, and keep your soul diligently, lest you forget the things that your eyes have seen, and lest they depart from your heart all the days of your life. Make them known to your children and your children's children."[4] Forgetfulness, Moses said, would be doom of God's people (as indeed it was).[5]

When the discipline of celebration is neglected, you are training yourself to believe that what you've done or experienced isn't important or worthwhile. The failure to pause and reflect on past successes creates a cycle of feeling like we are never enough, yet when your spirit is alive with gratitude and thanksgiving, you will become a life-giver to your family and workplace—one who remembers your community back together.

> The failure to pause and reflect on what God is doing creates a cycle of feeling like we are never enough.

When you accomplish something great, do you stop to acknowledge it or do you immediately move on to the next challenge? When something beautiful occurs in your or loved ones' lives, do you stop to take it in? When was the last time you created space in your busy schedule to practice thanksgiving and celebrate past wins?

In Scripture, celebration was planned and intentional. After the children of God were saved from the hand of Pharaoh and traveled miraculously through the Red Sea, Miriam the prophetess picked up a tambourine and led the women in a celebration dance. To celebrate the dedication of the wall of Jerusalem the

---

3   Naranjo, *Character and Neurosis*, 226.

4   Deut. 4:9

5   Isa. 17:10

Israelites recruited two choirs and rounded up the best musicians for a big party. Celebration and the remembrance of salvation past and ongoing was even written into their calendar! Ancient Israel was required to gather three times every year to celebrate God and His mighty acts through festival holidays. Likewise, the traditional church has followed Israel's lead, with a calendar marking seasons and days of expectancy, celebration, and confession.[6]

How will you plan to celebrate? Like the people of Israel who set up stones to commemorate their entrance to the promised land and set up days to return to the monument and remember, how will you lay your stones of remembrance? How will you create more space to celebrate both the past beauty and the new? Remember, to be a daily life-giver, cultivating an attitude of gratitude—of thanksgiving in remembrance—takes intentionality. As Richard Foster says, "The decision to set the mind on the higher things of life is an act of the will. That is why celebration is a discipline."[7]

The Good News for Peacemakers is that many of the practices we have already discussed are easily adapted to the task of celebration and remembrance. The church's calendar and our weekly gatherings are set up to help us remember with thanksgiving. Write about it in your journal and take time on retreats to remember. Gather with your community to feast, sing, and dance. Begin your conversations and team meetings with the question: "Where have we seen God working?"

→ Pray

Father, I bless Your holy name! You have forgiven my sins and redeemed my life from the pit. Your Son, Jesus, received a crown of thorns so that I would be crowned with Your steadfast love and mercy. By Your Holy Spirit, help me to never forget all You've done for me. Enable me to lead a celebratory life that rejoices in You always.

---

6   Examples: Advent is about expectancy for Christ's appearing; Christmas is the celebration of his arrival and revealing; Lent and Holy Week are the desert of testing and sharing in his passion; Easter is joy at his defeat of death with everlasting life; and Pentecost is celebrating the Holy Spirit's descent onto all creation.

7   Richard J. Foster, *Celebration of Discipline: The Path to Spiritual Growth* (San Francisco: HarperOne, 2018), 195.

Day 38 Reflections:

What are you celebrating?

How can you devote more time to the discipline of celebration?

How can you spend more time, personally or in meetings, calling out greatness in others?

→ Respond

Start a new tradition or rhythm of celebration and stick to it.

Day 39:

Don't Bury Your Treasure

His master said to him, "Well done, good and faithful servant. You have been

faithful over a little; I will set you over much. Enter into the joy of your master."

—Matthew 25:21

ADVIL IS A LIFE-SAVER ISN'T IT? WE take this over-the-counter medicine regularly to numb many of the nagging pains that come our way. A team from Ohio State did a study where 167 subjects were given either a dose of acetaminophen or a placebo and then were exposed to both negative and positive images. The subjects who took the real Advil not only described the unpleasant images as less emotionally arousing but also the pleasant images too, compared to the placebo group. The study concluded that acetaminophen actually weakens a person's ability to process positive emotions.[2] Peacemakers seem to have the ability to create the same kind of effect within themselves. When they numb themselves, they suppress both the unwanted and good emotions. As Dr. Jerome Wagner explains:

> You cannot find peace by avoiding life.
>
> –Virigina Woolf[1]

---

1   Cron and Stabile, *The Road Back to You*, 64.

2   Geoffrey R O Durso, Andrew Luttrell, and Baldwin M Way, "Over-the-Counter Relief From Pains and Pleasures Alike: Acetaminophen Blunts Evaluation Sensitivity to Both Negative and Positive Stimuli," Psychological science (U.S. National Library of Medicine, June 2015), https://www.ncbi.nlm.nih.gov/pmc/articles/PMC4515109/.

"Nines turn down their energy, stay calm, and don't get excited or upset. They are great levelers, making molehills out of mountains. 'Make straight the way of the Nine.' They don't let anything stand out, get focused, or become too important. Life and relationships become homogenized, generic, the same. There are no highs or lows."[3]

Their line of thinking goes like this: *Things will stay calm if I don't make a big deal about my emotions or express my needs.* This emotional flatlining is an attempt to curb the pain of life's worst, but it comes at a cost—by attenuating *all* experience, Nines are just as likely to miss out on the good as the bad. Ian Cron sums it up this way: "They literally don't want life to get to them. … They ask little of life and hope life returns the favor."[4]

This way of living is far less than what Jesus prescribed for you. He said that He came so that you may "have life and have it abundantly."[5] While your unflappable emotional stability is a great strength to yourself and your community, experiencing life in all of its fullness will be impossible with a "no highs or lows" approach to living. God gave your body dopamine and serotonin to provide adrenaline rushes and heighten your pleasure, and the same is true for your soul. God created you to live an exhilarating life!

The Parable of the Talents illustrates what keeps us from entering into the joy of the Master—a life of playing it safe. In the story, a boss distributes funds to three different employees

> Jesus expects a return on our lives.

before he goes on a trip. When he returns, the boss asks his employees what they did with the money he entrusted to them. The first and second employee doubled the value of their funds. The third employee, wanting to avoid the failure and disapproval that comes with risk, hid the money in the ground.[6] However, this "play it safe" strategy backfires when the boss returns and learns that the third

---

3   Wagner, *Nine Lenses.*

4   Cron and Stabile, *The Road Back to You,* 66-67.

5   John 10:10

6   Matt. 25:14-30

employee had not made the most of what had been given to him. He calls this employee "slothful."[7]

Peacemakers are tempted to bury it all—finances, emotions, dreams, and talents. Jesus entrusted us with all those gifts because He expects a return on our lives. He's not asking you to be impulsive, but rather to take the initiative to make thoughtful steps of faith that allow you to leave the world better than you found it. This fulfills humanity's mandate in Genesis.[8]

The Good News for Peacemakers is if you dig up the potential you've buried and put it to use, then you will hear the words, "Well done, good and faithful servant."[9] God's invitation today is for you to trade a life of numbing your emotions and experiences for the abundant life.

→ Pray

Father, in Your presence there is fullness of joy and at Your right hand are pleasures forevermore. Make known to me the path of Your abundant life, and I will follow.[10] Forgive me for playing it safe. Help me to walk by faith, taking emotional, financial, and spiritual risks just as Jesus did to make me His treasure.

---

7   Matt. 25:26

8   Gen. 1:28

9   Matt. 25:23,29

10   Ps. 16:11

Day 39 Reflections:

How has your emotional stability served you well in life?

_____

_____

_____

_____

How have you experienced the consequences of playing it safe?

_____

_____

_____

What people or experiences caused you to bury your treasure? Who can help you dig up your full potential and maximize it?

_____

_____

_____

_____

→ Respond

Identify one of the following that you'd like to invest more of yourself in: a relationship, new career path, neighborhood, volunteering opportunity, church leadership, or creative pursuit.[11]

---

11   Cloud, *9 Things You Simply Must Do*, 31-32.

Day 40:

Take The Stage

Mordecai told them to reply to Esther ... "For if you keep silent at this time,

relief and deliverance will rise for the Jews from another place, but you and

your father's house will perish. And who knows whether you have not come to

the kingdom for such a time as this?"

—Esther 4:13-14

WE'VE COME TO THE END OF OUR 40-day journey, and the final question I want to ask is: Will you take the stage? Will you resolve to go public with your gifts rather than stay out of the spotlight? Beatrice Chestnut explains that "Nine leaders typically don't like being the center of attention, preferring to 'lead from behind,' "[2] and Ian Cron agrees, adding that "Nines gravitate toward middle management where they can avoid the kind of conflicts and stress

> One of the worst things you can die with is potential. Die with failures before you die with potential.
>
> –Henry Cloud[1]

---

1   Cloud, *9 Things You Simply Must Do*, 41.

2   Chestnut, *The 9 Types of Leadership*, 283.

associated with leadership such as making unpopular decisions, supervising employees or having to fire people."[3]

Are you putting a leadership lid on yourself because of fear or self-doubt? Beth McCord found herself in this aggravating place for years. As leadership teams and churches called the McCords to teach on the Enneagram, Beth found herself saying, "Jeff, you do the teaching." On the inside, she thought her presence didn't matter. Jeff honestly thought that he was doing her a favor by not making her step into the spotlight. Years later, as Jeff looked back on that time, he realized he had been sabotaging Beth's leadership by allowing her to hide.

From 2008 to 2012 Jeff was the public face of this powerful marriage duo. Remaining hidden for so long eventually caught up to Beth, and she found herself in the car one day screaming at the top of her lungs. She

> You were not created to be the supporting cast in your own story.

says it was in that desperate moment that God spoke to her in a whisper: "Why are you so angry?" Beth responded, "Because I overlook myself. ... I've been hiding for 14 years."

Beth got out of the car and turned her anger into action. She took her newfound knowledge about building a leadership platform from working as a personal assistant to leadership guru Michael Hyatt and began to dream up *Your Enneagram Coach*. As of today, the McCords have trained 1,000 Enneagram coaches in 20 countries, have had over one million people take their Enneagram assessment online, coached thousands of individuals, and co-wrote the best-sellling book *Becoming Us: Using the Enneagram to Create a Thriving Gospel-Centered Marriage.*[4]

When I think of Beth's story, I'm reminded of the biblical leader, Esther. Through the machinations of the evil advisor, Hamon, Emperor Xerxes decrees that all the Jews were to be killed in every province. Esther's uncle, Mordecai, finds out about this plan and sends his niece—now Xerxes' Queen—a message: *plead for the lives of your people before the King.* If you keep silent, Mordecai says, deliverance

---

3   Cron and Stabile, *The Road Back to You*, 85.

4   Your Enneagram Coach, *Episode 1: The Story of Your Enneagram Coach*, podcast audio, April 14, 2020, http://you-renneagramcoach.yec.libsynpro.com/episode-1-the-story-of-your-enneagram-coach

will come about one way or another. He asks Esther to view her ascension as God's provision "for such a time as this"[5] for what would otherwise be a hopeless situation. Esther knows her life might end by making such a big request before the king, but she risks it anyway. As a result, the Jewish people are saved!

Make no mistake: you are just as wanted and needed in the world today as Esther was back then. You were born into human history "for such a time as this." There are still conflicts all around in need of a resolution in which God has sovereignly created you to strive. Within God's universal drama, there's a story He has written specifically for you. Get this: *you* are the main character. Don't be tempted to take yourself out of your own headline; you were not created to be the supporting cast in your own story.

The Good News for Peacemakers is that God says, "My grace is sufficient for you, for my power is made perfect in weakness."[6] Do you believe that? If so, it's time to roll up your sleeves. Don't leave your life to fate or wait for someone else to make the first move. Create the life that you want to wake up to tomorrow.

→ Pray

Father, I know You believe in me because I am Your beloved child, created with a purpose. Help me believe in myself. I know that if I abide in You, I can ask whatever I wish and it will be done for me.[7] So I'm asking nothing less than for You to change the world through me. Use me as a main character in Your unfolding plan to reconcile all things.

---

5   Esther 4:14

6   2 Cor. 12:9

7   John 15:7

Day 40 Reflections:

What's tempting about leading from the shadows rather than the spotlight?

When have you displayed a bold spirit in the face of danger?

How do you want the world to remember you?

→ Respond

Find a life coach or spiritual mentor to come alongside you to support you in accomplishing your goals. Start working toward something today that seems impossible without God's supernatural power and grace.

Prayer for Peacemakers

FATHER, I AM DEEPLY GRATEFUL TO YOU for creating me in Your image as Your child. You created me to specifically reflect Your peace and unity. I confess I've lived too often for the agenda of others, rather than seeking to please You alone. Ignoring my need for true intimacy, I have often numbed myself, masked my true emotions, and avoided working out conflict. I have settled for calm instead of pursuing wholeness. You, being rich in mercy, saw me from heaven and sent Your Son, Jesus, to die on the cross for the conflict I caused because of my sin. Now, I revel in the fact I've been forever merged with Christ in a relationship that will never be broken. Clothed with the power of the Holy Spirit, I will accept resistance as a normal part of life and leadership and will fight for peace. Putting off my stubbornness and self-doubt, and putting on my new self that is made in Christ's image, I will seek to speak up for myself, share uncomfortable truths, be zealous for good works, and pursue courageous transparency. Amen.

Next Steps

I'm so proud of you for finishing this 40-day journey. That's a big accomplishment! As I said in the introduction, this devotional has just as much to do with what comes *after* the 40 days as it does with what you've learned during the 40 days. You're probably wondering: *What now? My eyes have been opened, I've grown in greater self-awareness and empathy, and now I'm ready to take the next step!* Here are some ideas:

1. If you haven't yet, put your trust in Jesus. You can do this in your own words or by repeating the Prayer for Peacemakers on the previous page.

2. Download my free resource called *Should Christians Use The Enneagram?* at gospelforenneagram.com.

3. Ask a friend, spouse, or mentor to meet regularly with you to discuss the insights God has revealed to you through this book. Invite them, along with your small group, to get a devotional on their Enneagram type and share what they learn with you.

4. Join a church community where you can continue to grow in your knowledge of God and self. To go the distance, find a mentor, coach, or support system.

5. Follow "Gospel for Enneagram" on Instagram, Facebook, or Twitter to continue learning and engaging.

6. Visit our website, gospelforenneagram.com, to find more helpful links and resources.

7. Email me with any thoughts, questions, or feedback to tyler@gospelforenneagram.com. I'd love to hear from you!

Download my free resource called "Should Christians Use The Enneagram?" at gospelforenneagram.com.

Acknowledgements

My wife: Lindsey, you show me the gospel every day by loving me for who I am and not what I do. Thank you for your tremendous encouragement to be a writer and for bearing with my workaholic tendencies. I want to be more like you.

My editors: Joshua, thank you for bringing your incredible creativity to the table. Your re-rewrites helped elevate my writing to a whole new level. Stephanie, your attention to detail and passion for this project gave me tremendous confidence. Lee Ann, your veteran experience and thoroughness increased the value of this book tremendously.

My coach: John Fooshee, thank you for your Enneagram coaching and partnership. I'm deeply grateful for your willingness to come alongside me and put wind in my sails.

My influences: I wouldn't have been able to pull this off without a multitude of direct and indirect influences such as pastors, teachers, and writers (including you, mom!) over the years. I'm deeply grateful for the spiritual heroes that have come before me and shaped me.

www.GospelForEnneagram.com

Follow us:

 /GospelForEnneagram

 @GospelForEnneagram

 @GospelForGram

INTRODUCING

A DEVOTIONAL SERIES WITH SPOT-ON TRUTHS FOR YOUR TYPE.

Reformer

Helper

Achiever

Individualist

Investigator

Loyalist

Enthusiast

Challenger

Peacemaker

GET NEW BOOK UPDATES AT
GOSPELFORENNEAGRAM.COM

Made in the USA
Coppell, TX
09 September 2021